DEMONIC
Storm

My Life of Satanic
Deception and
Spiritual Deliverance

Kimmie Eichelt

DEMONIC STORM
Copyright © 2020 by Kimmie Eichelt

Back cover quotation from:
Lewis, C.S. 1996. *The Screwtape Letters*. Harper Collins: 1996, ix.

Cover Art by Kevin Carden at ChristianPhotoshops.com

Print ISBN: 978-1-4866-1906-1
eBook ISBN: 978-1-4866-1907-8

Word Alive Press
119 De Baets Street, Winnipeg, MB R2J 3R9
www.wordalivepress.ca

WORD ALIVE
—P R E S S—

Cataloguing in Publication may be obtained through Library and Archives Canada

Acknowledgements

Typically, the first acknowledgement is to Jesus Christ for all He's done, but if I haven't made that abundantly clear throughout this book—well, it shouldn't have been written at all.

Instead, here I'll acknowledge the folks on earth that God has graciously given to me.

My parents—*wow*—thank you for everything! For always loving me, always praying for me, always being there for me regardless of the crap I put you through. Thanks for all the support—spiritual, emotional, physical, and even financial.

My daughter—for your simple statement when at times I got overwhelmed recalling and reliving the past while writing this book: "Mom, did you forget to pray before starting to write again?"

My friends, friends of friends, relatives and co-workers/friends—your opinions and feedback helped me decide on cover art. I value all your opinions and appreciate that you took the time to comment and elaborate. And those of you who don't share my faith, yet still encouraged me on—thank you, and know I'm forever praying for you.

David, my original editor at *BeWriteThere* editing—thank you for taking my one long sentence with little punctuation (except those en dashes LOL) and turning it into paragraphs and chapters. You did an amazing job! While you don't share my faith (yet... I'm still praying for you too), you were most patient and kind even while challenging me.

Matthew, my finishing editor at Word Alive Press—you got me through the bland and mundane to completion, and most importantly—you did it while making me laugh. Thank you.

Prologue

What follows is a true account. It's my story. Before the actual account of my life begins, this is what I surmise happened behind the scenes. I can't claim it's accurate, but I'm guessing it was something along these lines.

The demon lord approached the throne of God and bowed (as every knee must bow in His presence).

"She is born. We have come to seek permission to have her," snarled the hideous creature.

"No, she is mine," declared the Lord of Hosts.

"By your own laws, by your own decrees, we have every spiritual and legal right to her through generational curses; your own words have declared it." The demon lord was now hissing, very much afraid of reporting failure to Satan.

"Yes, you have the right. You may have your way with her, but you may not take her life—it belongs to me; she is mine."

"We shall see," hissed the demon lord, "we shall see."

The demon fled the throne room fully armed, with the permission from the Lord every demon needs to operate, and headed to Earth to accomplish the mission.

Jesus laughed. He, the Holy Spirit, and God the Father, all in one, knew full well the outcome—they knew that although things would be dark, Jesus's work on the cross had already overcome it all. His own plan was already in action.

Chapter One

As a baby I was adopted into a Christian family, given up by a girl whose family was involved in the occult (something I would find out later). One would think the story ends here, but the whole Bible is true, so Exodus 20:5 came alive: *"...I, the Lord your God, am a jealous God, punishing the children for the sin of the parents to the third and fourth generation of those who hate me..."* My story doesn't begin and end without incident.

Shortly after adopting me, the Christian couple were killed in a car wreck. What was to become of their new baby? After lengthy court battles, the husband's brother, Henry—a single male from Edmonton, Alberta—got custody of me. Perhaps today this wouldn't be so strange, but fifty-plus years ago a single *male* getting custody of a baby girl was unheard of! This defied all the acceptable norms of the day. But God knew what He was doing! God knew ahead of time that Henry would be the only one open enough to the existence of the demonic to be willing to learn more about it—and, more importantly, pray directly about it.

I lived with Henry and his mom and dad as part of the God-inspired custody agreement in which Henry would live with his parents and all would be fine. It's interesting to point out that Henry was in his early twenties; imagine the God-inspired love that would have to infiltrate for a single twenty-year-old male to fight in court for a baby he didn't really know and then agree to continue living with his parents.

For me, it was a picture-perfect existence. Beautiful house, nice neighborhood, friends down the block, and of course, I went to church every Sunday. Perfect except for one thing—the black panther.

My room was at the end of the hallway, and from time to time I would walk by and see this large evil cat with glowing eyes sitting on the bed, growling at me, ready to pounce. This was terrifying! I would tell Henry and he would come and look, but whenever he was there it would be gone. I found some relief in this, but that stupid cat would still show up from time to time when I was alone, causing me to run back into the living room in complete fear.

I quit telling Henry because the evil cat never seemed to be there when he was around—I would just wait till Henry walked down the hallway and go to my room when I knew the cat wouldn't show itself. The cat was the only fear I knew then—but it was also only the beginning.

When I started Grade One, Henry and I moved to our own house. His mother had passed away, and while as a result the courts could have stepped in and started the whole process again, God had hidden all this away, as He did with Moses in the bulrushes, to ensure I was where He knew it was best.

The house was amazing, and I had the best of everything. Anyone looking in from the outside could see I was a princess, and was provided with nothing but the best. The only problem with the new house was that the panther had not only come along but had apparently gained strength. I not only saw it in the basement, but I could now *feel* the fear; I could *feel* the presence of evil, and it didn't only live in the basement. I would see glimpses of something upstairs and feel the chill down my back. While this didn't happen enough to mention it to Henry, it became an underlying fear that lived in me.

Throughout this period, though, I went to school, was happy, had friends, and was a top honor student. Life (other than the evil presence) was great. I went to church and knew Jesus loved me; I had accepted Him into my heart, and also knew of demons—although at that time they "only lived in Africa" and far-off places. The demonic wasn't something that the "civilized" folks in North America needed to worry about—a common demonic lie that still works.

I did all the normal things any kid did. I belonged to the chess club at school, went to the park with friends, watched TV, did my homework, loved every September when I'd get all the new school supplies, and, due to my voracious enjoyment of reading, was never bored. Life was great! Because it was just Henry and me, we ate out a lot; I knew the restaurants in town better than most adults did. Some of my friends would say they were a bit jealous of me—I truly had it all.

Chapter Two

In the summer between Grades Five and Six, I went to a Bible camp. I was so excited. It was such great fun—plenty of playing in the lake, numerous land games, and, of course, the evening hot chocolate and chapel time.

One evening, as we were sitting around with our hot chocolate, I happened to glance out the window and saw something evil looking directly at me. It was large and grayish and had eyes that glowed a ruby red. It was beckoning me with its finger. I screamed! The entire table looked at me as I pointed out the window to where this thing was looking directly at me. Unlike the panther, it didn't disappear when they looked; it kept its gaze on me, but no one else could see it. How could they not see it? It was as plain as day, and glaring directly at me!

The counselors thought I was nuts—either that, or desperately looking for attention. I was neither; I was simply horrified to my core. It took some time before they could convince me to actually go outside and walk back to the cabin, and even then I only ventured outside with my hands in a death grip around the two counselors who walked with me. This was just the beginning.

When I returned home, Henry had heard about what had happened, and while we talked about it, the spiritual reality of the situation hadn't been uncovered yet. Life continued, school continued, but in Grade Six, while I still had my regular friends and my grades were still in honor standing, things slowly began to change. The fear of what I'd seen never left me. I always remembered. While I still attended church and believed all the right things, an inner struggle was intensifying.

By the time Grade Six ended, my grades were not only on a slippery slide down, but I had discovered boys, and I wanted their attention badly.

The summer after Grade Six, I went to a nice Christian camp again. Don't misunderstand: I was more than excited to go—my heart still loved God, and I loved all the goings-on at camp—but my head had some opposing thoughts. Somewhere along the line I got the idea to have a séance.

Bad move—God was clearly not impressed with this idea. Leviticus 20:27 says, *"A man or woman who is a medium or spiritist among you must be put to death. You are to stone them; their blood will be on their own heads."* I am convinced that the generational curse on my life was beginning to bud and bloom at this point.

I went down to the lake with a few other campers after dark and began to "summon" different dead, departed folks. Things moved along interestingly enough until those same ruby-red eyes from the previous camp showed up. They were larger than before—and calling me to come from the middle of the lake. I felt a strange, eerie acceptance that I should go— wrap myself in the arms beckoning me, and be quietly taken to my death.

Okay, seriously—what young kid has these thoughts? I'm sure there was some little imp, unseen by any of us, whispering these ridiculous lies to me. To the dismay of my friends on the shore, I was determined to go; no one could hold me back. They eventually got some counselors out there to keep me from what would have been a midnight drowning. Surprisingly enough, some of the counselors at this camp acknowledged that séances were demonic and could attract demons—but this only piqued my interest.

At the camp was a counselor—Samuel—over whom all the girls were swooning. He was so cute! Something inside me was determined to "have him," although if asked I wouldn't have been able to elaborate on the desire. I made up stories of how wild I was and what I did (none of it true—yet!) to get him to "counsel" me. Oh, how the demons must have danced. He and I went off alone in the bushes so he could talk to me. Obviously he wasn't quite the Christian he claimed to be, since his version of "counseling" involved trying to get into my shorts!

I remember thinking, "This is exactly what I want... No, wait! Not what I want! Yes, I must have him! No, this is stupid! Yes! You must have him!" The battle in my head was ridiculous; the two opposing trains of thought were smashing head-on with each other over and over, and I was becoming confused. God stepped in; out of my mouth popped, "I can't do this to you, you're a Christian."

Samuel was clever with his quick recovery after what had almost happened, saying, "See? That shows you're not that far gone."

I know that only the prayers of his devoutly Christian parents, and of mine, stopped the demonically inspired sexual encounter. While they may not have been praying against the demonic specifically, both his parents and Henry were praying individually for the two of us, and I know those prayers alone are what stopped things.

When I got home from camp, neither the lake, the séance, the eyes, nor the bush encounter were ever mentioned, but something evil had not only taken root in me, but was beginning to grow. Leviticus 19:31 says, *"Do not turn to mediums or seek out spiritists, for you will be defiled by them. I am the Lord your God."*

Besides having a generational occult history, I had now willingly opened the door to demonic oppression and possession. Exodus 34:7 tells us that God is *"...maintaining love to thousands, and forgiving wickedness, rebellion and sin. Yet he does not leave the guilty unpunished; he punishes the children and their children for the sin of the parents to the third and fourth generation."*

That same summer I started hanging out with some girls I knew from the neighborhood. They were definitely from the "other side of the tracks," but something in me was absolutely drawn to them. They were as far from my regular circle of friends as they could be.

Alcoholic parents, parents who sold sex for money, parents who did drugs and didn't care one bit where their daughters were or what they were up to. With my demonic lenses in place, all I saw were friendly, fun-loving girls with enviable freedom.

One night they invited me to a party. A party? I'd never been invited to their type of party—I must be "special" for them to want me along. But there was no way on this earth I would be allowed out that late, never mind to a party.

What to do? The only way I could go to a party and get away with it would be to go and not go home—ever. The idea was quick; it settled, took root, and became my reality. I would run away to absolute freedom, never to return home again, and this party would be the beginning of my new life of fun and freedom. All of hell was celebrating.

We went to a small apartment. There were a few people there already, drinking and smoking drugs. My friends were known to them, and it appeared I was the guest of honor (little did I know...). When the host asked me if it was true I was a virgin, I was immediately embarrassed. He could see my embarrassment and took advantage of it by telling me, "Don't worry—it's okay, I can help you with that, I can be your teacher." Anyone with a normal functioning brain would have quickly turned and left—but in my demonic state, I was instead flattered and happy to lose this pesky title of virgin.

Things happened as one would imagine. It was not in the least bit pleasant. It happened over and over. Finally, when everything was done, I emerged into the living room where my friends actually clapped and cheered for me. All unpleasantness forgotten, my only thought was, "I belong. I'm one of them now."

Somewhere in the night I must have fallen asleep; my girlfriends had left as it didn't matter when they got home. When I woke up, I was completely and utterly alone.

I ventured outside the tiny bedroom and found chaos and loneliness. I walked into a dingy apartment with not one other living person. The "party palace"—all the music, all the drugs, all the laughter and people—was gone, replaced with a stench, a complete mess, and unbelievable solitude. The ashtrays overflowed onto the table, the drinks left sticky rings everywhere, and the half-empty beer bottles that littered the floor held remnants of the joints that had been passed around.

Never having been to a party, much less the aftermath of one, I was completely overwhelmed. My first thought was to clean up. My next one was to run as fast as I could from this place—the emptiness was swallowing me whole. I did the only thing I could manage at the time—clean up this crazy upside-down place.

Where was everyone? Where were the friends who were going to be "free" with me? Where was the party, the fun, the freedom? All that was left was a loneliness and a stench. I started picking up the littered bottles, and a new thought crept into my mind—the first of many God-inspired thoughts that would try to prevent me from walking this new path I found myself on: *Do you really want to live like this forever? Do you really want to be "free" to be scared, confused, and lonely all day just to relive the horrible night again?* As this thought grew, so did my panic and fear. What if the guy who owned the apartment came back? What if I could never leave? It was obvious my friends were long gone—but what if he came back? I made a quick decision and ran as fast as I could out the door.

Once outside, I realized I had yet another problem—I didn't have a clue where I was. I didn't know which way to run. What if he drove up and saw me? Who would I call anyway? I hid in an alley to collect my frantic thoughts. Okay, go home, face the music, and stay away from this place—wherever this place was. New problem—where was the nearest phone? (This was long before the time of cell phones, at a time when pay phones still existed on street corners and cost less than a quarter.)

I managed to slink through enough alleys, find a familiar location, albeit far from home, and find that quarter to call home. I was surprised that Henry didn't yell at me; in fact, he sounded happy to hear from me. Now, as a parent myself, I realize he was relieved that his night of praying had paid off and I was alive and calling home. Me, I was just happy not to be yelled at.

Home had never felt so good! Beautiful surroundings, no stink, no mess, and best of all, no loneliness, no feeling so lost. Something felt right. Strangely enough, that night Henry gave me the money to buy a leather jacket I'd been eyeing. Off to the mall I went; life felt normal again!

The first person I saw at the mall was Chloe—one of my friends who had urged me to go to the party—laughing at me and asking how last night had felt. She seemed rather amused, but I was outraged! She had left me in that sty of a place, and here she was laughing at me and asking if I wanted to party again—how dare she?

In hindsight, I can see that my invitation to the party wasn't an accident. I firmly believe my "friends" were paid in cash for delivering an eleven-year-old virgin to the party. Oh, how the demons must have danced. And their party was just beginning.

Chapter Three

I turned twelve and never spoke of the party again; nor did I want to hang out with Chloe and crew. Sadly, the transformation that had begun in me had wreaked complete havoc with my social life. I no longer fit in with the good honor students; my grades and, more importantly, my attitude were falling; and I didn't fit in with the popular kids.

Even though I looked much older than my age and was far more developed than most of the girls, I wasn't allowed to go to the "tamer" parties, which left me in a place I'd never been before—unable to fit in anywhere. I had a few friends, to be sure, but it was never the same.

I still went to church through all this. My neighbor and probably closest friend was Nadine; we would take the church bus to Sunday school together. Unfortunately, that's all we did—the moment we arrived, we'd skip out and go flirt with the boys who ran the corner store. They were more than happy to give us smokes and flirt it up. Needless to say, Sunday school didn't help us much; we only continued to go to keep Henry from driving me there—taking the bus, we could escape and be "popular" for a while.

While this made up my Sundays, school marched on. One day I heard some people talking about a guy who "fried his brain" because he sniffed an aerosol. Okay, some guy fried his brain and was in a coma—this would tell anyone with one ounce of intelligence that it was a bad thing to do, yet my intelligence had been demonized. I set out to try this aerosol thing for myself.

I came home one lunch hour—no worries of Henry being there, as he still taught elementary school and wouldn't be home—grabbed the aerosol can, and gave it a try. Instant high! Absolutely instant! I'd never experienced this before. The problem was that it only lasted maybe five to ten minutes; no wonder the other guy fried his brain. This was cool, though. I emptied my entire deodorant spray can that one lunch hour. Thank God for a praying parent, or I'm sure over the next while I would have fried myself into a coma as well.

Day after day, I lived to come home and use the aerosol. By now, smoking a joint—or five, or ten—was not an unusual event in my life either: a quick trip to the mall and I could find anyone willing to give a girl a high, especially one who looked like she was sixteen and was better at flirting than most professionals.

Had things continued as "normally" as they were, who knows what would have happened? My life was never going to be simply wrong—no, it had to be the demonic, full-of-evil type of wrong.

One lunch hour, I came home and was heading to my room when I tripped over something on my floor. In the split second of mid-fall I realized something was wrong—I hadn't hit the floor, yet I wasn't upright either. In my mirror, which faced the doorway, I could see myself halfway there, suspended in mid-fall (*The Matrix* before its time, but in real life).

I looked up from my not-falling fall to see a hideous dark creature holding me up! This thing had hold of me to prevent me from falling. Worse, it was the thing from camp! What do you do when your worst nightmare comes to life and stops you from falling? My mind wasn't ready for this any more than my eyes were ready to see it. It helped me upright, and had I not been so terrified I may have said, "Thanks."

Here was my worst nightmare, alive and well after all these years, and helping me. My head was spinning, and I was dizzy. This thing helped me into bed. I was so terrified I didn't even know what to do. I lay there wondering how this had happened, wishing beyond anything that I were stoned, since that at least would have explained this. Well, having been raised in a Christian home, I knew all about the name of Jesus, What the heck, I decided, let's give it a try.

As I lay there, I prayed. "In the name of Jesus, leave me alone."

What happened next was beyond comprehension. The room seemed to spin—a thousand faces all melding into a fog swirled from under my bed. Like a rushing river flowing from under my bed, the swirling faces kept coming or going (I wasn't sure which). I was too terrified to look anymore, so I hid under my blankets. Praying had done something, alright—although I still wished I was stoned so I could explain this better.

I managed enough bravery to peek out after some time and, the coast clear, resumed my otherwise normal school day, the picture of what I'd seen permanently impressed on my brain. For the rest of the day, it was difficult to focus, and I had a new fear of mirrors as I didn't have a clue what might suddenly appear in one.

That evening I wasn't feeling especially well; I suppose a close encounter of the demonic kind will do that to you. I didn't mention this to Henry as it was too unbelievable—no one would believe it. I was having a hard enough time believing it myself—oh, how I wish I had been stoned; at least then I could have rationalized it.

When I went to bed, I had another visitor—not as scary or as sudden as the earlier one, but rather an impish character, almost amusing in a way. He or she wore what seemed like large clown shoes, along with a dress and a nurse's hat. It came in, stroked my hair, said nothing, smiled at me—not even an evil smile, just a normal smile—walked back into the house, and faded away. I realized at that point that my visitors had never really left—they were there always, sometimes seen, other times merely felt.

School continued, and my marks continued to decline, my upbeat, outgoing personality slowly fading into more of a sarcastic, dark aspect. The drugs continued, rarely more than the "organic" type, and although they were certainly not hallucinations, my demonic visitors seemed more readily visible when I was stoned.

Chapter Four

I had one friend who seemed to have a fun, party type of life; her name was Liz. Like me, she had a parent in the school system: her mom was a teacher. Her parents were a little freer than my dad was, so I'd spend weekends at her place. We'd go out drinking and partying with the guys from around her place. She lived out on an acreage, so there was a lot more open private space to party, and as long as we were back by her curfew, our being drunk as sailors didn't get noticed. We'd party with the surrounding boys. We were only in Grade Seven, but these guys, they were older and cool, most of them in high school and able to drive. I discovered a new doorway into popularity: sex.

We'd go out, and if the boys decided they didn't want to buy more booze or take us where we wanted to go, a simple promise of sex had them taking us where we wanted to go or buying us whatever we liked. I never considered it prostitution, but a means to an end. The boys were so easy to fool, each thinking he was king of the hill and the best of the best. Stupid boys! They thought they were getting what they wanted, but we were getting what we wanted, and I really enjoyed being the popular girl, the one everyone wanted on the weekend. The parties continued, the grades fell, the demons danced.

While I still managed a relatively normal façade at home and even at school, albeit with a reputation slowly sinking to major slut status, I experienced a constant inner turmoil. Romans 7:15 says, *"I do not understand what I do. For what I want to do I do not do, but what I hate I do."*

The loneliness could be masked with more alcohol, while the emptiness could be temporarily alleviated by being desired and sought after.

Sometime that year, closer to the summer, Liz and I decided to run away and live our own lives. I packed my stuff, but she packed the whole house! She had everything from her clothes to her mother's brandy decanter (complete with brandy in it) to the $800 cash she'd stolen from her grandmother who lived with them. (That's around $4,000 in today's currency). Again, the stupid older boys with their trucks came in handy.

We had such fun shopping for an apartment; we looked at all kinds of furnished high-rise suites, and we could picture ourselves living the high life in one of them. We found an apartment, but met a girl, Barb, who said we could move with her if we paid only half the rent—why not? We unloaded my clothes and Liz's entire house into the little bachelor apartment. What to do now...

The first thing we did was shop. With that kind of money, we could go a long way. We bought fancy new outfits, makeup, and jewelry, and decided to be "high class." We went to the La Ronde, a prestigious revolving restaurant atop a hotel with a complete view of the city. We were dressed to the nines with far too much cash. No one questioned these twelve- and thirteen-year-old girls, since we came across as much older. We drank and drank and ate and flirted with the waiter and host. By the end of the night, we had not only drunk far too many free drinks but had acquired the phone number and address of the host. Of course, we "promised" to show up later in exchange for our free drinks; I hope he didn't wait too long as we had no intention of going. Instead we headed out to a nightclub.

Nights turned into days slept away with hangovers and headaches that turned into nights on constant repeat. No worries of how to continue paying for all this; our money hadn't yet run out.

Within a month or so, Barb—this new "roommate" of ours—was making a stink about how much money we'd spent without her. Who did she think she was? It was our money, and we'd already stocked her fridge full of food she wouldn't otherwise have had. We were heading out to go find another place to live when we met two guys in the elevator. We were complaining about Barb, and of course they offered us a "free" place in exchange for cleaning and "companionship." So of course we chose the new place and promptly moved our stuff from her apartment down a few floors.

This arrangement lasted comfortably a few weeks. Sex was no big deal; at this point it was simply a means to an end, nothing emotional or romantic. The cleaning, however—now that irked us. We partied and partied, but when we were expected to clean up, that left us angry. As it was, we'd blown through the money Liz had stolen.

To supplement our cash shortage, I would pick up a guy and take him back to the apartment for a fast fifty bucks or so. I had learned this interesting form of employment from my stint back with Chloe and her friends. Bringing men back for cash could get tricky as I lived with two other males and Liz. While Liz didn't concern them, should one of the guys be home, the trick would get nervous and leave. It was a balancing act, to be sure.

On one occasion, the gentleman wanted to talk a bit first. I was annoyed (time is money), but okay, let him talk—he'd already paid me. He asked me how old I was. I thought perhaps if I told him the truth, he'd pay me more money, but instead his words still ring in my head.

"My God! I have a daughter your age—keep the money. I need to leave."

I didn't make any extra, but I did receive payment for doing absolutely nothing, and who knows, perhaps God used that event to get him to go home, hug his daughter, and be a better husband and father. God never wastes anything. Regardless of what Satan attempts, God can use any situation to His glory. As Genesis 50:20 says, *"You intended to harm me, but God intended it for good to accomplish what is now being done, the saving of many lives."*

Eventually I managed to secure a job in a tiny place called the Waffle Shop, but it wasn't enough for our lifestyle, and bringing guys home was hit and miss with four of us living there. Okay, perhaps it was time to go home. Why not? We were basically out of money, and partying wasn't as much fun if you had to clean up.

By now I'd had a taste of no rules, and at twelve had decided that it was my right to continue living this way—even at home. So while Liz went home to her house, I went off to mine.

I told Henry how it would be. I fully expected him to agree; after all, he'd gotten his kid back. What more could he want? Yes, demons are stupid, and so was my thinking. When I told him that I'd be home but had no intention of going to school and would come and go as I pleased, he quickly brought me back to reality.

He said, "If you live here, it's under my rules—if you don't want that, then you'll have to leave."

Who tells a twelve-year-old to leave? A very smart man! If I'd stayed with Henry in my state, I would have had too much of a safety net and would never have reached the rock bottom of loneliness and fear it would take for me to cry out to God. After I recovered from my shock, I thought I'd call his bluff. I told him I was leaving. Yeah, that should bring him around.

Wrong! Instead, he handed me $20 ($80 today) and told me to use it for dinner, wished me good luck, told he loved me, and said I could always come home when I was willing to live by the rules. The story of the prodigal son comes to mind, doesn't it? (Luke 15:11–32)

Chapter Five

I left, finding myself very lonely and confused back downtown in a little restaurant—and I had no Liz for companionship this time. The despair wasn't enough to drive me home; the loneliness and fear weren't enough either. Instead, in my demonic state I simply sat until the place closed and wandered the streets till I found someone to spend the night with. By now I had discovered that the demonic that seemed to hound me day and night could also be used to my advantage. I was not at this point formally into Satanism, but I knew enough to be dangerous. I knew enough to understand that something powerful was in me, and in a tight situation I could have it manifest in order to scare people away. This became very evident to me in one of my living arrangements.

I was housing myself in a rundown apartment at the bottom of a hill off Jasper Avenue. I lived with an epileptic man who needed help; he was also living with another teenager, Micky. I suppose he was as lonely as we were, and we were all good company for each other. As twists would have it, I knew Micky from the Bible camp where I'd met my first demon. To be sure, neither of us was one of their success stories.

Micky was enterprising. I found out he was selling information about me and my whereabouts to Henry. This didn't sit well with me, so I told him I would use the occult to pay him back. He didn't believe me. But one night I was trying to contact a demon to throw something at him, and when I looked up, he screamed! He was terrified at what he saw superimposed over my face. He ended up huddled in a chair unable to move, all the while horrified at what he'd apparently seen. I'd seen nothing, but knew I must have some form of power. I actually believed I controlled it—not the other way around, which was closer to the truth.

I moved out of that apartment to stay upstairs with a guy who thought he was so powerful because he could read tarot cards. This actually amused and also mildly annoyed me, as I "knew" I had the real power, not him.

I had also become familiar with a nightclub downtown. Originally, I had snuck in the back way to ensure they wouldn't check my ID. While I was always mistaken for someone older, this was a popular club, and even the "old folks," those twentysomethings, had to show their IDs. Once in, I made a point of getting cozy with one of the bouncers. We spent a few nights together, so after that getting into the club was never a concern. I would waltz in, maybe go home with someone, maybe not, but I never had to worry about buying my own drinks; there were enough men around willing to pay for booze in the hopes of taking me home. Again, drunken nights turned into lonely days. I was turning the odd trick for money, and nightly getting drunk to forget the squalor I was living in—and on it went. Life was one dismal existence.

One morning I actually woke up before noon. The loneliness and despair were killing me, and being awake I couldn't shake it. I was so upset that I went to a seedy little bar downtown and at eleven a.m. promptly started drinking screwdrivers. I was sad and beyond miserable and quickly becoming drunk. I looked at my surroundings—old derelict people who reeked of booze, dressed in ratty clothes, and all doing the same thing I was doing. Okay, now I wanted to go home. How could I do this and still save face?

An idea: I would call the police and report a minor being served and acting rowdy in the bar I was at—that would bring them in, and surely they'd find me and arrest me and take me home. I could go home without admitting I wanted to so badly. So I sat and waited for the police to arrive. They soon did, and they looked around but didn't come to my table. What in the world was going on? I wanted to be taken home! Okay, so let's get this show moving.

I swaggered up to the police and asked what they were doing there. To my shock and horror, they said, "Ah, just a report of a minor being served and drunk in here."

Hello? That's me! I screamed in my head, but not out loud. I couldn't believe I was right in front of them, yet they didn't give me a second glance. Now how in the world could I go home?

In the end, God allowed a strange situation to happen to get me home. It could all have ended a dozen other very ugly ways, but again, Genesis 50:20 was proven to be true: *"You [Satan] intended to harm me, but God intended it for good to accomplish what is now being done, the saving of many lives."*

As I was sitting there, a much older lady approached me. She was missing a tooth and reeked of booze. She chatted me up a bit and invited me to her room. Yes, I could certainly have used a nap and some time to gather my thoughts, I thought to myself.

We went up to her little piece of hell in this hotel. She was asking me all kinds of strange questions. Had I ever been hurt by a guy? Of course, who hasn't had their heart broken? But then she started rubbing my back and chest, and pulled my shirt up and off while telling me how things would be different with her, a woman! Okay, now it was time to leave; she absolutely freaked me out! I used the excuse that I had to go to the washroom first (which, to give you an indication of the type of place I was in, was down the hall). I took off and never looked back. I went home with my tail between my legs.

I wish I could say this was enough to cause me to give Christ a second look, but no, whether I was in control of myself for a few moments or not, I still had my demonic entities that were constantly at war with me and my own mind.

Chapter Six

I returned to school for Grade Eight; because my marks were always so high, I was moved up to Grade Eight even though I hadn't fully completed Grade Seven.

I was actually happy to leave behind the lonely world I had been living in and return to safety and a form of normality, going to school and living at home. I didn't discuss with my school friends where I'd been or what I'd been doing— none of them would have understood at all, much less believed me.

Midway through the year, however, my reputation caught up with me: SLUT written in black pen across my locker and all kinds of innuendo thrown my way. I'd made it through Grade Seven and the beginning of Grade Eight—but now, threats to my popularity were growing in ugly ways. I fell from the sought-after girl who would *probably* "put out" to the disgusting girl who *always* did.

For the remainder of Grade Eight, I was moved to an academic school across town. After all, I'd once had honor grades; get me away from the "bad crowd," put me in with the academically advanced kids, and I (and my grades) would return to normal—or so it was thought. What no one had yet factored in was that I was taking my demonic entities and influences with me. I'd already opened the door with my sexual exploits and drug use, so while I may have changed locations they came right along with me, inside me.

My first day there was a monster success in my twisted world. When the principal took me in to introduce me to my new class, a guy spoke up, saying, "Oh, we thought that was your girlfriend!"

I thought, *So I look old enough to be the principal's girlfriend, eh? Okay, I can most definitely work with that.*

While I flunked most of the classes, I certainly passed "being popular"—the boys wanted the girl who looked like the "principal's girlfriend." Interestingly enough, these "good academic kids" were most certainly advanced; yes, they knew how to cheat on tests, they knew how to make films—pornography—and they came from well-to-do families, so they could afford higher quality drugs. I snickered inwardly the day the police came to do their regular "be good and stay out of jail" speech to the schools and actually said, "We realize it's not a problem here, but we need to talk about it anyway." It was hard not to laugh out loud. Of course they weren't getting arrested for drugs or such there—these kids were smart, and far too privileged to get caught! Things are not always what they appear to be.

For the part of the year that I did attend the physical building called *school*, my time there was spent getting dropped off at the front door and walking straight through to the back door to head out and get high for the day. There was a ravine close by, and we'd head down there and get stoned and watch the clouds form interesting shapes.

I always hung out with the older kids, the Grade Nines. One in particular, Teresa, became a close friend. To look at her with her blond hair, proper clothes, and the almost refined way she had about her, you'd assume she was the best-behaved kid. Again, things aren't always as they appear.

She helped me cheat on papers (although I still failed due to lack of attendance), and she was smart—incredibly so!

There was a winter camp at Oak Bay—yes, the Oak Bay where the demons almost dined on a counselor. It was during a weekend over Halloween. I wanted to go, and I was taking a friend; Teresa had agreed to come.

So what happens when you take a demonized backslidden kid and a clever non-church girl to a Christian camp for the Halloween weekend? Well, the costumes Teresa brought were of band members from KISS—a band just gaining popularity then, and as far from a "Christian" rock band as could be. We dressed up and appalled and shocked everyone.

I was reveling in the negative attention. I also watched as Teresa took to task the counselors who tried to tell her about Jesus; she came at them with both barrels blazing, and they weren't ready for her type of arguments as they were just volunteer kids only a few years older than we were.

When I got home and told Henry about how she had made the staff members look foolish, he just looked at me and said, "Why are you so happy about that? You believe in Jesus. I thought you wanted her to as well."

I was stunned; the question seared my brain. It was a fair question and true—why indeed was I so happy about this? The question actually shook me to the core, but only for a few brief moments. For those few seconds, I was actually sad for her. The part of me that knew and loved Jesus was sad and extremely confused, but again, it was too short-lived.

I existed in two diametrically opposed worlds: one, in which I spent relatively little time, as the thirteen-year-old Grade Eight kid who knew about Jesus, and the other—more prevalent—as the demonized hell-bent disaster I was. Like any normal Grade Eight kid, I had friends from school come to sleep over, I watched the "right" TV shows, and I worried about being popular, but I also went out on weekend-long parties drinking, getting stoned, and sleeping around. My two worlds kept colliding.

Once again, my demons were getting restless; it was time to leave, as Henry was beginning to wise up to the demonic creature in his own home—perhaps because he'd been having encounters with them manifesting through me from time to time. He had started researching, and better still (or worse if you're demonized), he was praying specifically against it. God never wastes anything. In Henry, He was raising up a giant of a spiritual soldier.

While the demons were dancing, thinking they were harassing Henry, God was in control, using the circumstances to immerse him in the art of spiritual warfare.

Ephesians 6:12 says, *"For our struggle is not against flesh and blood, but against the rulers, against the authorities, against the powers of this dark world and against the spiritual forces of evil in the heavenly realms."*

This was a truth the churches chose to avoid or completely ignore at the time; it was during an age when they thought demons "only lived in Africa," but Henry was finding out that the reality was different. Today, churches are a little less oblivious to the spiritual warfare around them—a *little*...

Chapter Seven

It was time to go find and "have" that counselor from camp from years ago. This time I knew what I was doing; I wouldn't be pretending. I had become well versed in sexual destruction.

I would go to British Columbia. I had no fear, only a demonic drive to get there. I left home yet again. I stayed in Edmonton a few nights, robbing a few men of their dignity while they paid me for the privilege—like lambs to the slaughter. They were easy marks who paid morally, emotionally, and spiritually for a few short moments with me, but of course, all I cared about at the time was that they paid financially.

I hitchhiked my way west across Alberta, through the Rockies, and into a small town in BC's Fraser Valley. I would find a friendly trucker who simply wanted someone to talk to for his portion of the trip, or a desperate foolish man who would also pay for dinner, the motel, and breakfast the next morning. How cheaply a man will sell his morals, conscience, and body for a few minutes of pleasure, but I didn't care at the time—they were all fools. They may have looked at me and laughed and thought "slut" or "whore," but from my perspective they were all the same—weak and willing to hand it all over for a few moments of lies.

I was beginning to think all men were stupid and weak. I had demonically learned how to control men through sex. This is not typical thinking for a thirteen-year-old; in fact, nothing I've written should be considered typical. The only thing typical about this situation was the destruction left behind by demonic interference—this is all they do, and they are well versed in it.

I made it to small-town BC and promptly looked up my counselor. Now I would finish what was started years ago at the camp, and there would be no stopping me this time. When I called him, I was shocked to find out he lived with his parents. What a disappointment. This would make it more difficult to "have" him. Nonetheless, never one to be slowed down, I headed on over, determined to find a way.

When I arrived, I was a little taken aback at the size of the house; it was magnificent! It had a long, winding driveway, a deck overlooking a mountain view, numerous bedrooms, and a backyard that was more like a campground. It even had a pond, complete with ducks. It was simply beautiful—breathtaking. It turned out the large house was not only magnificent, but housed other troubled kids.

At dinner that night, I not only met the houseful of kids they had, but my counselor lost his appeal for me. Samuel was no longer the "man" I had to have. Seeing him in his environment made him just an older kid who lived at home with his parents, though he might still have been fun for a night or two. The other thing that happened at dinner was this: I discovered his parents were born-again Christians. This was probably why they took in so many kids and why their own son would have been involved in a Pentecostal Bible camp. Ha! If only they'd known the truth about their son. I chuckled inwardly at the thought.

I spent a few days and nights there. I would go out to the yard in the grass and by the beautiful pond. I reveled in the peace I found; it was beautiful when I was out there alone with no one around. The annoying part, however, was that I was finding it next to impossible to get the last of the over-sixteen males alone. Worse than that, I was extremely uncomfortable inside the house when Samuel's parents were present. I couldn't put a finger on it, but my nights weren't restful, and time spent with his parents left me seriously on edge. They were very sweet people who were annoying me out of my skin for reasons I couldn't quite explain.

I decided to get even with them for whatever they were doing that was making me so on edge; I'd show them. I put a curse on them one night. I asked for them to be terror-filled and horrified, and to know it was me who had done it.

This was not one of the smarter moves made through me by my demons. That night while the other girl, Tira, and I were in our room, we heard a noise. We both woke up—wide-eyed and breathing heavily—to the sounds of marching, and in the doorway to our room were a pair of boots, doing just that: marching. To say terror filled the room would be beyond an understatement. Tira looked at me, eyes wide, and simply said, "I'm too scared to breathe." She promptly hid under the covers and got close to me.

Me, I didn't have the luxury of hiding—the horror was like a fog I couldn't escape. The boots marched, and the terror continued. For how many hours I sat transfixed I don't recall, but I do know at some point I must have been allowed to fall asleep. How do I know this? Because I woke up in the morning—one has to be sleeping to wake up. Tira and I exchanged that look—the look that says "If we don't talk about it, then it never happened."

I went downstairs for breakfast. Samuel's mom looked at me, and with a smile that said she knew full well what I had done, said, "Did you have a nice night, dear?" Okay, how in the world could she have known? She took it a step further and went on to say, "Dear, don't you know you never put a curse on a blood-bought Christian because it just bounces back to you?"

What was this? I'd never heard such a thing! And further-more, I'd never told them or anyone what I had done; how had she known? I had (incorrectly) assumed I was invincible, and that I held the power. What was going on? Psalm 109:17–19 tells us exactly what was going on.

> *He loved to pronounce a curse—may it come back on him.*
> *He found no pleasure in blessing—may it be far from him.*
> *He wore cursing as his garment; it entered into his body like*
> *water, into his bones like oil. May it be like a cloak wrapped*
> *around him, like a belt tied forever around him.*

On Sunday they informed me we were all going to church—apparently this was a weekly ritual that was never avoided. Okay, I'd been to numerous churches; this shouldn't have been a problem, right? Wrong!

It was bad enough that I was on edge around Samuel's parents, especially with his mom knowing about my "curse," but when we pulled up to this church my stomach turned ab-solutely sour. It was churning and gurgling, and I was dizzy. While I couldn't explain it, I thought perhaps my reaction would be reason enough for them to take me home, right?

Wrong again! They hauled me into church. I immediately ran to the bathroom and began throwing up. Something in me told me I had to get away from there—and fast. I turned on my heels and ran straight back out the door and down the road. The farther away I got, the better I felt. As I got away from that place, I began to settle down again and not feel so anxious. I had no idea at that time that the demonic within me couldn't stand the power of the living God exuded by that place—a church in the 1970s that was totally spirit-filled and knew about demons. Who knew that type of place existed? I'd certainly never encountered an issue going into a church before.

The family found me wandering roads I was completely unfamiliar with in this mountainous community, and they took me back home to their place. I noticed a smile on the mother's face. Here it was again—that "I know something" type of grin.

Regardless, I finally managed to get alone with Samuel. We were in his bedroom, and he told me he wanted me to hear a song. He started his cassette player, and while I don't recall what was playing, I remember an incredible rage coming over me as I reached over to smash the machine.

He looked at me with astonishment. He wasn't nearly as astonished as I was, though. What was happening? Why was I suddenly enraged and trying to smash this device? I couldn't explain it, but then it got even stranger...

I walked into the open area of the house and was about to leave. An urgent scream inside me was telling me to leave, and that's what I intended to do. Samuel came in and basically restrained me, but this wasn't good, and I had to get out!

His mother came down the stairs, and out of my mouth came, "You called him, didn't you?" Let me repeat: out of my mouth came, "You called him, didn't you?" It wasn't a cognitive thought. My own ears were hearing what my mouth was saying, but my head wasn't thinking.

She just smiled at me, and even Samuel looked confused. He asked her who I was referring to, and again, out of my mouth came, "She called the pastor." This was getting bizarre—my mouth kept spouting stuff that I could hear, but my brain wasn't telling my mouth to say it. She affirmed that was what had happened.

Somehow I managed to break away. *Run, run, run,* was all I could hear in my own head, so run I did. Down the road I ran; they followed me in their car, and still I ran. My demons took a turn down a dead end (God controls all—even the direction the demons would turn). The car followed.

I found myself in a bit of a bind: dead end one way, car full of Christians the other (not that I fully understood why this should be a problem). Suddenly it was as if something had grabbed me, and I found myself wrestling in the grass with some unseen force. Okay, now this was getting even crazier; there was nothing there, yet I was being scratched and pulled and scraped by this "nothing" in the grass. The only actual escape would be to go with these Christians. I chose the latter, and back to their house we drove.

Well, the pastor didn't show up, but these two people knew enough about the demonic realm and deliverance to decide it was time to pray for me—and pray they did. Strange things were happening, as once again my mouth began speaking words I wasn't thinking, and there was also a murderous rage in me.

I was terrified beyond belief. Here I was, a thirteen-year-old girl caught in the middle of a spiritual war that I didn't fully understand. I barely even knew this kind of spiritual warfare existed, yet something inside of me was reacting to it as though I knew full well what was going on.

I can't honestly say how long this went on for, but at the end of it all I felt empty and somewhat lighter. Something was definitely different. I couldn't figure out why I didn't have the confidence in myself and my own "power" that I used to have. I felt like a rag doll who'd had the stuffing removed, and while I felt lighter, I also felt empty and sad. I didn't accept Christ after this.

God bless those people; they did temporarily evict my demons, but without Jesus filling the void I was left in a more dangerous place.

Now is a good time to point out—the Bible is extremely clear about this. According to Matthew 12:44–45,

> *Then [the impure spirit] says, "I will return to the house I left." When it arrives, it finds the house unoccupied, swept clean and put in order. Then it goes and takes with it seven other spirits more wicked than itself, and they go in and live there. And the final condition of that person is worse than the first. That is how it will be with this wicked generation.*

This is exactly what happened to me. Through the power of the name of Jesus and His shed blood, Samuel's parents were easily able to have the demons evicted from me. This isn't a problem; the name of Jesus carries all power and authority in the spiritual realm, and the "house" (my body) was now clean, swept, and in order. Truly a massive cleanup had been done inside me. However, because I wasn't at a place where I was ready to give it all to Jesus and surrender to Him (I can't even blame the demons this time—just my own stubborn human nature), I was unoccupied. No Holy Spirit, no Jesus taking up residence, just a clean yet empty "house." Be sure of this: whatever they evicted did in fact go, did find evil spirits that were more powerful and evil, and did return to take up residence in me. Yes, I was actually worse off than before.

Days went by without me doing anything extremely stupid or drastic, but I was quickly growing bored and restless. There was nothing to do except listen to these folks drone on and on about God, listen to their old-time Christian music, or walk the grounds. One day I decided I might as well hitchhike around and see what kind of fun I could drum up.

I left the area and a pickup slowed down, so I quickly hopped in. The minute we started driving, I could feel something wrong. There was something ominous and unsettling about this fellow. We didn't drive to a motel or even to town. We just drove the mountainous roads in the area. He talked to me quite nicely, asking me questions about where I was staying, what I did for fun, that sort of thing. By all standards a very normal conversation, and nothing to worry about. For reasons unknown to me, though, a terror was building in me each passing moment.

I thought, *Okay, I'll summon my powers from before and scare him if he gets weird.* Yet somehow I knew they were no match for him. How did I know this? Where did that thought come from? My heart was about to beat out of my skin. I finally turned to him and said, "You're the devil, aren't you?"

He turned to me and smiled. "Why do you say that?"

I had no answer. The only answer was in my head because this was a terror I'd never felt before, and something inside me also knew I couldn't contend with this person and his power. I believed I would die that day.

We started back to the house, and it was then he said, "You should be playing with Barbie dolls."

That statement would stick with me and come back to haunt me many years later. He pulled up to their house and got out of the truck.

He smiled and said, "I'm their neighbor."

I looked off to the side and saw a nearby house with a chair on the porch; interesting that I'd never noticed that house before. Relief and embarrassment flooded me: relief that he wasn't going to kill me as I'd felt sure he was going to, and embarrassment for feeling so helpless and powerless with someone who was merely the neighbor.

My relief from that day turned into complete confusion after a few days when I asked these folks about their neighbor. There was no neighbor! There was no house with a porch and a chair! I went back and looked; sure enough, there was a run-down house, but obviously no one had lived there for quite some time. This wasn't the house and porch that I'd seen just days earlier. Was I losing my mind? I knew what I had seen and experienced—the truck, the driver, the conversation, all real—yet no neighbor, no house.

Chapter Eight

Soon afterward, I got put on a plane home to Henry. I was actually relieved to be leaving that place. Samuel aside, being there had turned me inside out, and I had no idea of the true spiritual battle being waged behind the scenes.

So back home—to at least some form of normality. School was out by now, and once again I hadn't completed the grade. Again, because I was so highly intelligent (although given my actions one might question this), I would be moved up to Grade Nine the next year.

I spent the rest of the time waiting for Grade Nine to begin being "normal." I would go to church, but I never felt sick or needed to run out. Sadly, that was an indication of the state of the church; they may have been preaching Jesus and salvation, but for me to be able to attend without any issues shows the lack of spiritual power they were drawing upon. I went to the mall, hung with friends, got stoned with friends, and of course read lots of books.

I believe the demons in me had come up with a new strategy—stay under the radar and no one will notice. I was bound up demonically anyway; my thinking was corroded and my life was a wreck, so if they quietly manipulated me from inside without the outward manifestation... well, they could comfortably stay where they were. This is a strategy they still use to keep people in bondage to this day.

From all outward appearances, I looked like a normal teenager; I dressed like one, talked like one, and did most of the regular things teens do. Inside was a different story—I felt great turmoil, anger, fear, and also a craving for more evil.

Grade Nine began at yet another school, with me always trying to outrun my past and reputation, yet taking the very thing that damaged them along with me. I made numerous friends—the regular kids, the ones who simply drank, smoked pot, and slept with each other—for no other reason than emotional longing.

～

I had an interesting English teacher, Mr. Skila, and we had a double English period once a week. He thought it would be interesting if we were to study something different in that second weekly class; he wanted us to "get in touch with our inner power" and learn to levitate. The class, of course, all agreed—a bunch of fools buying into his ideas of having the power within to make things happen.

I knew better. Levitation—which he described with big, puffy, wordy New Age ideas—was nothing more than a piggyback ride on a demon. I couldn't believe how completely sold he was on what I knew to be demonic, and how the entire class could buy into this. Oh well, at least he didn't complain when I missed those classes. He was indoctrinating the class in the New Age movement, in white witchcraft. I was having no part of it: I believed in calling a spade a spade, and if he wanted to teach demonic doings and try to dress it up or make it sound light and fluffy, I was done.

Around the same time I was also taking drama, an optional class in the school. We did lot of New Age-type exercises where our teacher would have us lie back, close our eyes, and visualize our spirit guide. Nothing more than baby occultism for summoning a demon. I was okay with this because at least she was honest that we would meet something—at least it wasn't the hokey "power within."

One day after class, our drama teacher, Ms. Jem, came up to three of us girls and said, "I can see you're searching for something more and would like to help."

Hold your horses. No, she didn't go into a nice speech about Jesus and His love for us—quite the opposite.

She said, "Here, girls, this is for you—it should help you in your search," and handed us a copy of *The Satanic Bible.*

Wow, *The Satanic Bible*! Now we knew we were onto something! Our drama teacher saw something in us that no one else had; we were obviously quite special. We never talked to her about it again, but we did go to Julie's house on a regular basis to study and read it and try to do what it said, at least as far as conjuring up demons was concerned.

My nights were getting worse, full of all sorts of nightmares and terrors. The beings that I had once seen and grown used to were now starting to get mean. I no longer seemed to be their friend; rather, it was like they only showed up to terrorize me. I recall one night in particular I awoke feeling scared. I thought perhaps I'd get up and turn on a few lights to chase some of the fear away, but instead I was violently pushed back down onto my bed, unable to move, let alone get up. What was this? *I* was in control—they were supposed to listen to *me*, not shove me around like this. I was angry and scared. I did manage to drift off to sleep, and had the most horrifying sexual dream that I was being raped by something.

I was relieved to wake up to the bright sun shining into my room until I went to sit up and discovered a thick over-sized Sharpie shoved deep inside of me. Wait, it was only a dream, right? I didn't know anymore, and really didn't want to spend much more time thinking about it. Too much time thinking made me a wreck, so I developed the habit of quickly dismissing things and moving on. I tossed the Sharpie into the wastebasket and proceeded with my day.

Once again, I wasn't attending school, but rather wasting my life, getting either stoned or drunk or both and staying away from home for days or weeks at a time, only to return for a few days, regroup, and do it again.

I do recall one of Henry's attempts to get help for me. He sent me to a psychiatrist downtown, my old stomping ground. What the heck—I did attend a few times. I would show up, tell the man a few stories just to keep him wondering, let him give me his utterly useless advice (he was trying to help from the natural level, but my issues were supernatural), and after the hour of complete boredom I would walk to the nearest bar, have a few drinks, and head home (chewing lots of gum to cover the booze and cigarette smell). This arrangement only lasted for maybe three or four visits. Finally, I suppose, the psychiatrist had had enough. He actually said to me, "You're wasting my time here."

I was indignant! Wasting his time—*his* time? What about the hour out of my day I could have been partying?

I told him, "No, actually you're wasting my time and also my money."

I turned, walked out of his office, and never returned. I don't know what he told Henry about the meeting, but we didn't discuss my going back again.

By now, school was basically out of the equation, although I did try to complete Grade Nine by correspondence.

This was going okay until an English course assignment. We were to write a descriptive story. I wrote one, alright: it was very descriptive and detailed about a sexual fantasy. My paper was mailed back with possibly the first ever mark below an A I had ever received—it actually sank to B status—and a note from the teacher to "try to be a little more discreet next time."

There would be no next time. How dare they! Be a little more discreet? They wanted descriptive, and I gave descriptive. It never even dawned on me that at thirteen years old what I was writing probably belonged in an adult magazine, not a Grade Nine English paper, but then again, my life in no way mirrored a thirteen-year-old Grade Nine lifestyle. Actually, what I wrote was quite tame compared to what I had already lived. This was the end of any attempts to complete school.

Chapter Nine

A gain, days turned into months while I lived my two-person identity—the kid at home and the demon-driven wild child. I'd come and go from home, running away when I wanted to party a little longer, coming home when a small something in me craved normality.

At some point I ventured into a bustling pizza place called Hawaii Pizza. It was always packed, the jukebox was always full of tunes, and a lot of happening people were there. I decided it would be fun to waitress there. Why not? I had nothing better to do. As my life would have it, of course I was given a job. I had been pulling off an older façade for years now. No one questioned my age there either. I picked out a nice short skirt and high heels, and away I went. Tips were amazing, and while I didn't make quite as much as I had in my other profession, this was actually fun. More like being paid to party and keep it going all night. I would go home with whomever happened to be there the latest, and that's how I had a place to live.

Through all this, I know Henry continued to pray. That I'm even alive today attests to this.

God used strange happenings to reach out to me. One night I answered the phone at the restaurant, and someone playing a prank sang, "Witches, goblins, ghosts, and ghouls, dontcha wish you'd gone to school?" Although this may just have been a prank call, I was a bit shaken when I hung up. School, friends, honor student, nice house, and normality. Oh, the thoughts raced through me! I actually missed it, and for a brief moment considered walking out and going home. Of course, being so demonized by now the thought was a passing one, but to this day I remember what could have been a turning point in my story.

I became friendly with a group of guys who frequented the place. They were all in their early twenties, and they all drove fast cars. They were so much fun to wait on, and they always joked and were just full of life overall. One in particular, Marcus, seemed to take a liking to me, and the teenager in me was so excited—a cool older guy (although not so old as to need to pay me to be with him) who had a decked-out car and an apparently fun life wanted to know me better. After work he took me for a ride in his car; we raced up and down the streets, and it was quite a rush! Then he asked where to drop me off at home.

Hmm, okay, now this was a problem. I had no home, as such; I just went home with whomever was convenient, or sometimes with one of the waitresses who knew my real age and would put me up from time to time. But now, what to tell this guy... I couldn't let him know I was a fourteen-year-old runaway. I had him drop me off at one of the twenty-four-hour restaurants, explaining to him I needed time to myself to unwind and didn't want to have to cook my own breakfast. He dropped me off, and after making sure he was gone I called a cab, took my bag (with my few pieces of clothing stuffed in it), and headed to a motel.

He started showing up every night, and it was becoming more and more difficult to make up excuses as to why he couldn't just take me to my house. It never crossed my mind at the time how odd it was that he didn't invite me to his place like everyone else did. All I cared about was that he was cute and had a cool car.

After too many nights of having to pay for a motel, I finally told him that I was actually "between places." He must have figured something didn't sit right, and he started asking too many questions. I caved, and after I finally told him I was fourteen and a runaway, he said, "Why don't I drop you off at the coffee shop, and I'll be back in a few hours and we can go to my place?"

Well, that sounded much better. When we got to his place, after I'd sat drinking too much coffee for hours, I discovered why he had waited until late to take me home. My big hero lived with his mother! Sound familiar?

He had waited till she'd gone to work to bring me over. This should have told me something. No, again, in lieu of a functioning brain that would ask why a twenty-one-year-old who lived at home with his mother was interested in a four-teen-year-old, my mind twisted it in such a way that I believed I must be so beautiful for him to go to all this trouble for me.

This went on for quite a while. I also became close with Louise, another waitress from the pizza place, who really was over eighteen. She and her boyfriend managed an apartment out in the west end and told me I could stay in one of the vacant suites for free as long as I kept it clean. Well, hadn't I arrived! Now fourteen and working full-time—although I didn't consider it work, more like a big party that paid me to show up—and now I even had my "own" apartment. This was life!

This too was short-lived, as Louise's boyfriend saw Marcus for what he was, and they insisted that either he stop coming over with me or I had to go. Of course, by now I was "in love," so the idea that he was a leech didn't sit well with me. I cut my ties with them, and Marcus and I looked for an apartment together.

Interestingly enough, by now his mother knew about me, and yet she wasn't concerned that her son was dating someone who was well underage. It's worth noting that Marcus never seemed to hold a job long. He would work for a week or two and quit. Of course, he could always justify why he'd quit, and I, being the good girlfriend, always agreed that he was too good for that particular place of employment. Basically, I became the major source of income. I wasn't working the streets anymore; it's laughable, but Marcus had just enough morals to think I shouldn't be sleeping with other people while I (at age fourteen) was sleeping with him. Our income was based mostly on my minimum-wage job and tips, plus any income he would earn from his one- or two-week working stints.

We managed to secure an apartment: a dingy little walk-up, but it was ours. We had one chair in the living room, a mattress in the bedroom, and a little ten-inch TV. His mother gave us dishes, but given our lack of funds we didn't buy groceries, so we had no use for them. My meals were eaten at whatever restaurant or bar I worked at, and I'm sure his were eaten at home with his mother. Once a week we would go together for dinner at his mother's apartment.

When we did have extra money, it would be wasted going out to eat or on car parts for his car. Wasn't I cool? Oh, if my friends could see me now! From my view, I had the cute boyfriend who drove a fast car, my own apartment, my own job, and no rules. Yes, this was good.

At this point I didn't have much interaction with the demonic realm, but then again, why would they try to scare me or impress upon me to do something more evil? They already had me. I was living a pathetic existence and going to hell, so there was not much point in their manifesting; it might well have scared Marcus off, or perhaps even scared me enough to return home. No, their strategy was clever—sit quietly hidden inside, blind my thinking, and let me self-destruct. No one looking in would have said, "Oh my! She must be demonized." I was just another loser living a dead-end life.

The same problem exists today. While Christians are quick to recognize the demonic when it's in the form of something outwardly obvious or blatantly occult, the Church also needs to wake up to the very real possibility of the demonic being a little more subtle—think of that person you know who is always so angry, or depressed, or whatever.

Christians are too quick to write off people as having "issues" if they can't see the occult in the immediate forefront. I'm not saying every depressed or angry person has a demon, but while demons aren't all-knowing (they would have never left heaven willingly to follow Satan if they were), they aren't stupid, and they know how to hide and manipulate from behind the scenes if it allows their existence to go unchallenged.

My world continued on pretty much the same day by day, until I found out I was pregnant. I had a regular doctor's visit scheduled. I had time to kill first, so I bought myself a skimpy new outfit and headed on in. When the doctor told me I was pregnant, the first words out of my mouth were, "How did that happen?"

Of course, I knew how it had happened, but I meant that it couldn't happen to me. And my next thought was, *Oh no, that new outfit won't fit me much longer.* Another indication of how twisted my thinking was. I wandered around for most of the day in a daze. Pregnant? Now this was certainly an interesting twist.

God used my shock to speak to me loudly. As I wandered aimlessly downtown, my thoughts went back to home—to a nice house, nice neighborhood, real furniture, my room, going to school, even going to church. All at once I realized this baby in me would now have an eternal future. Did I want to raise a baby in the squalor and filth I lived in, or did I want this baby to grow up in a "normal" environment? What about God? Would this baby ever know God? If not, then hell was its only option.

Okay, seriously, what was completely lost on me that day was that all the worry and concern I had for this baby I should also have had for myself! My own eternity was at stake, but all I could think about was this baby not living the lifestyle I was living. Decision made.

"Hi, Henry—can I come home?"

Chapter Ten

Well, of course I could come home.

Henry showed up at the four walls I called an apartment, and against all Marcus's ridiculous cries of protest, we packed my few belongings and went home. Home had never felt so good. The nice big house, my beautifully furnished room, and, well, normality.

Now, I'm quite convinced that if my demonic issues had also been dealt with, I would have stayed home, and this story would be different. You can take the girl out of the filth, but if you don't take the filth out of the girl, she will return to it. In the words of 2 Peter 2:22, *"Of them the proverbs are true: 'A dog returns to its vomit,' and, 'A sow that is washed returns to her wallowing in the mud.'"*

Although things were outwardly better, my inner filth still existed. I still had seven times more evil demons in me than before (Luke 11:26), and they were now working overtime inside me to counteract the positive environment.

While home was good, I still felt the need for my own place. After having been gone so long, living at home—while normal and peaceful—just wasn't sitting right. I needed to get my own place, but this time somewhere nice, a real apartment with a real life.

It was at this point I found out I was entitled to an inheritance. Henry's brother and sister-in-law, who had originally adopted me and been killed—it turned out their entire estate fell to me.

Henry worked with the public trustee to get me a monthly allowance so I could afford my own place. He moved me into a nice apartment downtown and bought me furniture for it, and I brought my bedroom suite from home. The place was lovely and had life to it, as opposed to being a dingy box. The issue, however, was that I was lonely again.

I had long since lost contact with my school friends. There was the odd one I could talk to, but they were worried about final exams and school dances and all the normal stuff I had missed out on while I was getting as big as a house and had to worry about fitting through the doorway. I had no Christian friends, as I hadn't been to church in years, so TV and boredom were my constant companions.

I got so bored that calling Marcus became the only option in my limited thinking. He was happy to come and sleep over at my beautiful apartment; I suppose it beat being back at his mother's apartment, where he was living again. I fooled myself into thinking we could maybe have a life together. Maybe he could get a job and actually hold it, and we could be that family unit. He and I lived together off and on during the pregnancy. When he would annoy me or get abusive with me, I would simply kick him out. It was my apartment, after all; he wasn't on the lease.

I did try to reconnect with Liz, my friend from years ago, but by now she was living with some fellow and only wanted to party. Being pregnant, I didn't have the energy I used to have, and just wanted someone to come and watch TV with me. She was still going strong, and the last time we talked was when she said, "You've become so boring." I was devastated! I didn't want to be boring. I wanted to party, but I was so tired all the time.

The night I had my daughter showed just how young and naïve I was. My water broke at the apartment, and I thought I had wet the bed! I was so disgusted with myself. I went to the bathroom to clean up, and again, a surge of water. I was so confused; I wasn't peeing myself, yet where was all this moisture coming? Then the cramps started—aha! This must be what labor was all about. I called myself a taxi and went to the hospital.

At the admitting desk, I was in for quite the surprise: because I was underage, I needed parental consent to be admitted! Are you kidding me? I was in wet sweats from the water continuing to break, or maybe starting again (I wasn't quite sure); I was beginning to have cramps—and they wanted parental consent! I hadn't had consent when I'd gotten pregnant, but they wanted me to get it to have a baby?

Well, fortunately, I did know how to get ahold of Henry: he would be at his girlfriend Annie's house for dinner (she would eventually become his wife). Henry and I had our relationship back, and although I wasn't at home, we were in constant contact. I managed to get in touch with him, and they took me to a room. Eighteen hours later, I held my daughter, Nadine. She was beautiful—so perfect!

In the hospital, there were forms and more forms to fill out: mother's name, father's name, etc. But something in me didn't want to give Marcus that much involvement, so I simply wrote "father unknown." This brought a lot of interesting looks from the nurses on that day, but I think somewhere deep down I knew I'd eventually need to make a clean break.

A week later, I got a ride home while I held my daughter in my arms (this is long before the days of mandatory car seats). I arrived to find my cupboards stocked to the brim with baby formula—enough for at least two months—numerous boxes of diapers, and more than enough clothes to take her into the terrible twos. Henry and Annie had gone above and beyond in stocking my apartment and making it comfortable for me.

My new reality was interesting. I had all the furnishings of a normal middle-class life, but I was still lost. As a new parent, I never knew what to do next, and this baby didn't exactly come with an instruction manual. When Nadine would cry at all hours, and giving her a bottle or walking her around didn't help, I didn't have a clue what to do. It was easy for the week in the hospital; I only had her for a few hours a day, while the rest of the time the capable, knowledgeable nurses had her. Now, alone in my apartment, I was at a loss what exactly to do. Somehow, though, I managed to muddle through.

I still had Marcus over from time to time, but he became more and more abusive, and he still wasn't working steady. Once again, I was supporting him. There was one night in particular when not only was he abusive to me, but he grabbed Nadine and ran out with her. Of course, he ran to the only place he could go—to his mother's. I banged and banged on the door while inside I could hear him screaming with his family and my daughter wailing. Some neighbors of his mother's had called the police, and when they showed up his sister was yelling, "He has the scissors!"

I could only imagine what was going on inside, and my imagination was scarier than any truth. The police finally managed to get into the apartment and retrieve my daughter for me. I was so outraged, so angry, that over and over I told the police and Marcus, "When I turn eighteen and get my inheritance, I will pay it all to have you murdered!"

The police kept advising me to shut my mouth, but I kept telling them the same thing, and at the time I meant every word—I would have paid it all to have him murdered. Was this enough to oust him from my life forever? No, I was still too stupid, or demonized—or both.

Within a few months, however, he was proposing to me. He went so far as to say he needed to marry me before I turned eighteen so I wouldn't take off on him. For the first time in many years, I made a smart decision—to never marry him. Despite the idiocy of not completely throwing him out of my life, his proposal did finally push me to the point where I knew this was not a forever arrangement. I didn't end it quite then, but deep down, the knowledge that our relationship would be temporary settled and finally took root.

One afternoon a social worker happened by to see how I was doing. I still don't know who or what prompted her visit—perhaps it was yet another God moment. She sat on the couch chatting with me, and I rather enjoyed her company. She asked about future plans and what I had in mind. She also asked Marcus what he was going to do.

He replied, "I'm looking for a job."

Without hesitation she came back with, "No, you're not; you're looking at the TV."

I burst out laughing at her statement of the obvious; the simple truth of what she'd said hit me instantly. He was outraged! He started yelling at her, and the more he yelled the more amused both she and I became. Eventually he stormed out, and that social worker and I had a wonderful afternoon talking. By the end of her visit, I had decided something—it was time for Marcus to become history.

Given his temper, I had to tread carefully, and I finally formulated a workable plan. As he slept one night, I slipped my apartment keys off his ring and replaced them with keys that were the same shape but didn't open anything apartment-related. When he woke up the next morning, he headed off to work; fortunately for me this was one of his short stints at holding a job. I walked him down to the lobby in case he had any reason to need to come back up, as I knew his keys wouldn't work. My heart was beating double time. I needed this to work!

When I was sure he'd left and wasn't coming back, I raced upstairs and packed the few belongings he had accumulated at my place. I then called his work to say, "We're going to your mom's place for dinner, so go straight there from work—don't come home first."

He received the message, so I waited till later in the afternoon and called a taxi. I took the box of stuff, along with a note saying I was sick of him and his abuse, and that he was no longer welcome at my place or in my life, and shipped it to his mother's apartment. I had to wait, as I didn't want it arriving there early enough that his mom would open the box or letter and alert him.

It worked. About the time he should have been arriving at his mother's place, my phone started ringing and ringing; I didn't answer it. I ignored my phone for two days. Once, he must have gotten into the building with someone else, and I heard him banging on my door. I sat horrified in my apartment. He was there for hours, but I wouldn't answer; I just kept still and kept Nadine from crying, so he wouldn't know I was home. He eventually left.

Well, if this could happen, I had to move. Henry helped me secure another apartment in a different part of town. I was watching over my shoulder the entire move. I didn't want Marcus to see me moving and follow me. He had threatened to go to court and take my daughter, and told me that because I was a sixteen-year-old who used to be a prostitute, he would win. He had me convinced this could happen, so I had to be extra careful to disappear without him being able to find me.

When I got into the new building, I even bought new curtains so Marcus wouldn't recognize them if he should be driving by. Talk about paranoid! The odds of him being in this other part of town were slim enough, but to actually recognize my curtains! But I wasn't going to take any chances; he had me scared.

Chapter Eleven

Through the couple years of being with Marcus, it appeared that my occult history was long over. It never came up—at least it never manifested in the physical sense—and now in this lovely middle-class apartment everything looked normal. But my "house" was anything but in order. Just as in the natural realm—because a person doesn't have obvious skin lesions doesn't mean there isn't cancer present and spreading through the body—it's the same in the supernatural realm. I still had never addressed my demons, and they were still there, spreading their poison through me.

During this time, I sometimes worked and other times relied on my monthly inheritance check. I went back to old habits and brought men home off and on, but because there was now a baby involved it was a bit trickier. First I had to pay and get rid of the babysitter, then I had to hope my baby was sleeping and wasn't crying, all while knowing this could ruin the financial moment. I still managed to have gentlemen in and out occasionally.

The landlords of the apartment were Melody and Roy. Nice enough couple, although Melody could be a tad annoying with all her preaching and morality. But still, they were tolerable. After all, they did rent to me in a time when rentals were near impossible to secure, and there I was at sixteen with a baby—yes, I could tolerate her sermons while I brought men in and out.

I had decided I was done with the occult—it was no longer a lifestyle I wanted to be involved in. It had been a long time since the nightmares or visitations, and having been raised in a Christian home, I knew it was wrong.

Let me say now—knowing what is wrong isn't enough! Not doing blatantly occult things isn't enough! Knowing about Jesus isn't enough! James 2:19 says, *"You believe that there is one God. Good! Even the demons believe that—and shudder."* So all my "knowing" was for nothing. I still hadn't made Jesus Lord of my life.

One particular afternoon an old friend from way back came over. We talked at length about the past, but when she wanted to discuss her new involvement in witchcraft, I simply said, "I don't do that stuff anymore." Our coffee chat turned out okay, but something was uneasy in me.

Again, let me say that knowing about Jesus isn't enough. That night I got a firsthand taste of what the seven sons of Sceva got when they tried to cast out evil spirits in Jesus's name without having an actual relationship with him. Acts 19:13–16 tells the story:

> *Some Jews who went around driving out evil spirits tried to invoke the name of the Lord Jesus over those who were demon-possessed. They would say, "In the name of the Jesus whom Paul preaches, I command you to come out." Seven sons of Sceva, a Jewish chief priest, were doing this. One day the evil spirit answered them, "Jesus I know, and Paul I know about, but who are you?" Then the man who had the evil spirit jumped on them and overpowered them all. He gave them such a beating that they ran out of the house naked and bleeding.*

After my friend had left, there was a chill in the apartment. I don't mean the temperature dropped; I mean a "hairs standing up on the back of my neck" sort of chill—the kind I remembered from my earlier years when something made an appearance. I shrugged it off at first—after all, I wasn't participating in anything anymore.

The chill continued, and I was a little nervous. My daughter was cooing and playing on the floor beside me. I went into the kitchen to grab something when all of a sudden the dishes in the dish rack started to rattle and shake around. Okay, I know a demon when I see one, so in my "seven sons of Sceva" wisdom I said, "In the name of Jesus...." That's as far as I got.

My dishes were now moving out of the dish rack into the air! Suddenly, Nadine was screaming. I looked back into the living room, and there she was being stretched by unseen demons. Her legs were being pulled one way, her arms were over her head, and she was screaming. Well, my attempt at praying had only made things worse; now I was terrified! In my mind came the thought to grab my fanatical landlady, so I ran out of my apartment and started banging like a crazed person on her door.

Melody had obviously been sleeping, and there, answering the door, was this little five-foot lady rubbing her eyes and standing in her flowered housecoat and big fuzzy slippers. She just looked at me and said, "Oh, you have demons in your apartment" as calmly as one would say, "The sky is blue." I didn't care how she knew—although I was shocked that she did—but she came back to my apartment with me.

When she got there, she did something that horrified me to the core, yet God allowed her to impress upon me His awesome power. Melody walked into my apartment and said, "In the name of Jesus Christ, get out of here!"

Nadine stopped crying—her arms and legs no longer being pulled by the unseen demon—my dishes stayed still in the dish rack, and the chill was gone. This was enough to satisfy me, but no, as tenacious as Melody was, she took it one step further, declaring, "Satan, if you're so big and tough, materialize *now*, in the name of Jesus. I dare you in the name of Jesus Christ to show yourself now, if you dare."

Was this woman nuts? I was honestly waiting for the floor to open and swallow her whole; to pray and calm things down was one thing, but to actually dare Satan to show up so she could show him who had more power? Melody was playing with a fire bigger than her. Or so I thought...

What happened next was... nothing. Absolutely nothing. No Satan, no dishes bouncing around, no Arctic chill that meant demons were there—no nothing. I almost fainted in relief!

I was stunned at how she could pray those words and have the demons leave and peace restored. I couldn't even speak.

She then turned and looked at me and said, "It's time to stop playing games with God."

I was so shaken up I could only nod in agreement. Now, had she also prayed with her power and authority in Jesus that anything in *me* be gone too, her night of praying might have gone on much longer. While Melody had clearly evicted all the demonic entities in my apartment, those housed within me directly were still sitting fearfully quiet so as not to be addressed, probably quivering, thinking this little woman (by the power of Jesus) may well be about to take them on too—but their tactic of silence worked.

When Melody announced she was going back to bed, I grabbed her and begged her to stay. I called Henry in the meantime, asking him to please come get me. I had absolutely no intention of spending another night in that apartment—she may have prayed that stuff out of there, but I wanted nothing further to do with that specific apartment—ever! He did pick me up and we went home, but as I had been on my own for so long and now had a baby, it made more sense for me to still have my own place. Melody worked it so I could move out of that particular apartment and move into one on the floor above, so while I stayed in the same building, at least I wasn't in the same suite.

Enough of the weirdness—I wanted peace and normality. There's an old saying: "No Jesus, no peace; know Jesus, know peace." Very true—yet instead of Jesus, I decided that maybe working a typical Monday to Friday nine-to-five job would give me what I was looking for. I enrolled in a nighttime typing class.

Today, the same is true: people search for fulfillment with their jobs, their material possessions, their spouse, and their kids, but it's never enough. Jesus is the only one who can bring peace and wholeness to a person.

Melody (my landlady) and my daughter

Chapter Twelve

I enrolled in the evening typing class, thinking that maybe typing skills would come in handy trying for a "regular" job. It was a small class, and I met and became friends with another girl, Josie. One night after class, Josie and I were leaving, and the road was quite busy, difficult to get across. I told her not to worry, and that I would stop the traffic. I stepped out on the road and hiked my dress up all the way, uncovering everything right up to my neck. Needless to say, the traffic stopped. She laughed, and we crossed the street. We became close class buddies after this, and would sometimes have coffee together after class.

One day she approached me and said, "My boyfriend and I have always wanted a threesome; would you be interested?"

Well, of course I would. Why not? Sex was nothing to me—a means to an end, or just a boredom killer. I told her to bring him by that week.

When they arrived, I took charge completely. I told them both to get in the tub—after all, they did need to bathe if we were going to have sex. I ran a bubble bath for them, and sat on the bathroom counter talking to them while they sat in the tub. They both seemed awkward and nervous, which didn't make much sense to me since it was their idea, but I shrugged it off as them not knowing me that well. I marched them into my bedroom, and again they seemed quite taken aback. As things turned out, her boyfriend was so freaked out that the three of us couldn't function. After a lot of nothing, I suggested that perhaps it wasn't a good idea that night. They seemed more than happy, and almost relieved to be leaving. No harm, no foul; I wrote the night off.

The next typing class, I joked with Josie about her non-performing boyfriend. As friends often do, I ribbed her about her sex life and satisfaction. It was then that she came clean, and we had the best laugh ever. She told me that after my little performance stopping the traffic, she had told him about it, and because I had "freaked her out" by doing that, they decided to "freak me out" in return.

The whole threesome invitation was nothing more than their attempt to shock me. She told me that she almost fell over when I said yes and invited them over. She went on to tell me that they had circled my block a few times that night, smoking joints to try to relax before they came up. Apparently, the hope was that when they did show up, I would back out. When I ran the tub and told them to get in, they didn't know how to back out and save face, so that's why they got in. That also finally explained their apprehension and lack of... anything.

The two of us laughed and laughed. We sat there almost rolling on the floor about the whole episode. In thinking back, that was probably the night we became best friends. I found out Josie was from a town outside of Edmonton, and was staying with a family friend while she attended school. She didn't much like it there, as they were Mormons and quite strict—no smoking, no drinking, and certainly no boyfriend.

I had a solution for her: she should move in with me. I had a large one-bedroom, and we could share the room with my daughter and her crib; she could do whatever she liked, and we'd have each other for company.

She took me up on my offer. Her boyfriend became history. He was shocked and horrified that she would move in with someone like me. Not to mention, I'm sure he was too embarrassed to come over. So here we were, two sixteen-year-olds living in our own apartment.

Josie wasn't as open or free about sex as I was, but that was okay. She was still on the "normal" side: monogamous when it came to sex. That didn't bother me; she didn't judge my lifestyle, and I didn't concern myself with hers. To celebrate the new roommate situation, I went out and bought a few bottles of champagne. I still had my monthly inheritance checks, plus whatever I made through waitressing or other things.

We went on a three-day/night champagne fest. Needless to say, we'd quit the night classes by now. Sad to say, yes, my baby daughter was there throughout the partying. I introduced Josie to a number of men in the building. I knew a lot of them because I was easy and they were stupid. I particularly liked the married guys. I took great pleasure in having them over and seeing their wives in the hallway and acting as if I was their friend. To me, it was a game to see how many husbands I could get to stray while maintaining a fake friendship with their wives. Josie wasn't quite ready for the married guys, but there were a few single ones around too. My demons had managed to pull her into a new world of free and very casual sex.

Josie and I became inseparable. I would frequently hire a babysitter to stay the entire weekend at my apartment, and Josie and I would head out to see what we could find for fun. One night we were driving around, and I pulled off my shirt. I had her hike up her skirt and stick her legs out the window. We coined the phrase "boots and bras," and that was our new mantra. Boots and Bras: that's how we referred to each other.

Josie was working in offices through temp agencies, and I had a job waitressing from seven a.m. to three p.m. I would leave for work around six a.m., while Josie would get Nadine ready and take her to daycare for me. This worked perfectly for me, as I had to be at work when the daycare opened and she didn't have to be at work till nine. Josie and Nadine would pop over to where I worked, and I would get breakfast for both of them, although Josie typically only had coffee. She would then take Nadine to daycare and head to work herself. I would pick up Nadine from daycare and head home, and Josie would arrive a few hours later. We spent our evenings laughing, playing cards, sometimes getting stoned, and watching TV. A strong bond had formed between the two of us.

She told me about a best friend of hers who had died and how she was contacting her. I freaked out! I told her all about Jesus and the demonic and how she was basically communicating with a demon in disguise. This horrified me; I didn't want a repeat performance of my dishes going crazy and the bizarre happenings in the apartment. We did come to an agreement that she wouldn't practice her séances anymore, as they were wrong.

How much like Christians in general is this today? How much is this like the Church? Churches teach against the occult and homosexuality, yet they wink at those cheating on taxes, and turn the other way when husbands abuse their wives or children; they can justify sins that are acceptable to society or somewhat hidden, yet condemn those that are more blatant or obvious. James 2:10 says, *"For whoever keeps the whole law and yet stumbles at just one point is guilty of breaking all of it."*

It's not a matter of cherry-picking what suits us or allows us to continue in sin; God wants all of us, not just the parts we are comfortable giving to Him.

Josie and I fell into this demonic trap as well. Once again, I wouldn't have anything to do with the occult—but I continued having affairs with married men and casual sex with single men, and of course, kept using drugs. Unfortunately, I pulled Josie down into the same spiral.

We drank, we partied, the demons danced. One morning in particular, I found myself sitting, party dress on, bruised to no end, on the stairs inside the apartment. I was a little confused: First, why was I sitting on the stairs? Second, where did all these bruises come from? Third, and most importantly, what was going on?

I walked to our apartment and found Josie sitting at the kitchen table. She wanted to know what had happened; I would have loved to give an explanation, but I didn't have a clue where I had been or how I managed to look like I'd gone thirteen rounds with a pro fighter. The only thing I could remember was going to someone's apartment within our building, and the biggest detail I could remember was there was a fern plant hanging in the bathroom.

We never spent too much time trying to figure things out—we'd just brush problems off and move on, so that's what we did. But as a result of that night, I did end up in the emergency ward a week or so later, because whatever I had been with had left me almost unable to walk.

When the doctor said, "Oh my God!" and then called another doctor over to see whatever he was observing, I came to realize things were extremely bad, and it got me thinking back to the night I couldn't quite remember. Again, this should have given me pause, but no—my well-hidden demons were still in control, and despite not being able to walk and having to take pain medication, I continued down the same path.

We moved frequently from apartment to apartment all over the city. When we'd had enough of one place, we would move to another that always seemed just a little better. We always shared a bedroom with two beds, and my daughter would get the other. Josie and I had no issues being in bed with men right beside each other—we weren't shy, and had no inhibitions.

A new demonic turning point came for me one morning. I woke up with a young man whom I had taken home the night before. As he woke, he reached for me, and out of my mouth came, "Hit me!" He laughed and thought I was kidding.

I wasn't. "Hurt me, hit me," I kept saying; even Josie, three feet away, was a bit shocked. The kid wouldn't comply, so in a tirade I told him to get himself out of my apartment.

After he left, Josie asked me what I was doing. This was completely out of character for me; it wasn't something either one of us had ever thought of, let alone demanded. For the life of me, I couldn't explain this sudden overpowering desire for someone to physically hurt me. At the same time, though, I barely questioned it.

Being the best of friends that we were, she didn't question it either; she just shrugged and accepted that I was now into some kind of kinky sex. No big deal; she would do things her way, and I would do them mine.

⁓

We both ended up working in a pizza place in the evenings. I overpaid babysitters to be there from six p.m. till whenever we happened to be home. This was our "fun" time. We would go shopping during the day for matching outfits to wear that night and head on in. We were the life of the party. It was just the two of us working, plus a cook. We had a little game we played to see how much booze we could sell or give away through the night. Roger, the owner, wasn't around much at all, and given the shoddy accounting that generally was done back then, he gauged his success by the amount of empty booze cases and bottles that would be left. We always had a full restaurant of regulars; our deal was "Buy three beers, get a fourth free." You'd be amazed how many people would order and pay for six just to get the two free ones. We didn't ask for ID—a laughable thought, since neither of us was eighteen. Guys would bring in their underage girlfriends, knowing there would be no issue having them pumped full of alcohol. "Buy three, get a fourth free."

Josie and I had 'success.' Cases were regularly
stacked well over five feet high

As for men, I had found one who would temporarily satisfy my newfound desires. His name was Frank, and he also worked at the pizza place—he wasn't bad-looking, and was certainly built well. I went to his place one night and told him exactly what I wanted. He thought I was joking, and I made it quite clear I wasn't. What he did next should have turned me right around—but it didn't. He threw me down and held a knife to my throat and yelled, "Are you stupid? You don't even know me. I could kill you! You need to wake up and drop this nonsense! You can't ask strangers to hurt you!"

Without my demons, I'm sure I would have quickly agreed or ran out of there or something remotely smart—but no, still under demonic influence, I waited till he put the knife away and screamed back, "You're not a man, you're a mouse, you can't satisfy me! You're nothing. I'm leaving!"

Josie and I working halloween

I must have hurt his pride, because rather than let me leave, he accommodated me in what I was looking for—thankfully without the knife. I continued to see him for hookups for a number of months; he was now also beginning to enjoy this demented, demonic type of sex. Again, to put it in context, this wasn't your run-of-the-mill kinky sex. It was the difference between mild spanking and approaching sex like a King of the Cage[1] fighter.

Between Frank and our party job, we loved going to work. We made so much in tips that the actual paychecks we got were more of a joke. Everyone knew us and loved us. We would crank up the jukebox and encourage folks to dance in between the tables or even on the tables. If things were too quiet, one of us would start dancing. Occasionally, Roger caught us, but he was smart enough to leave quickly as he couldn't argue with the incredible sales of booze. We basically turned it into a bar that happened to serve pizza.

Getting the party started

1   UFC-style fighting, but without the rules

Josie and another customer table-dancing on Halloween

This arrangement became strained when I finally did turn eighteen. Josie, being my best friend, decided to throw me a surprise birthday party at the pizza place. She invited a number of regular customers and the daytime waitress whom we had become friends with. With a full array of friends, she brought me a bottle of our favorite champagne from the cooler. When Roger came by and asked what the occasion was, without thinking at all we announced that it was my eighteenth birthday, and we were celebrating.

Since we'd worked there for over a year and sold and served more booze than the average bar, it came as an unwelcome surprise to him that we were underage. He was incredibly angry. He could have lost his liquor license, yes, and his whole restaurant could have been closed down, but this wasn't a concern to Josie or me; we actually laughed quite hard at the whole episode.

We giggled all night over our mistake in letting him know we were underage. While he insisted that we weren't to come back, we weren't worried; for every waitress there were twenty jobs back then. We really didn't care.

Chapter Thirteen

I saw an ad in the paper one morning for an escort agency and convinced Josie that this would be the easier way to make money. While she wasn't yet "selling" sex, it was at least a casual happening now. We both went to work there.

Again, I would overpay babysitters to have them arrive around six p.m. and ship them home around six a.m. We were both making rather good money, but as my car wasn't working at the time, it was beginning to cost more in taxi fares and agency fees than it was worth.

We both tried our hand at this for a while, but I was quickly becoming annoyed with the whole setup. The agency demanded a fee for each call we went on, whether or not anything happened, and then there was the taxi fare both ways, so between taxis and the agency wanting their cut, it could turn into a hundred dollars or more that I was giving away. No, I could make better money working the streets. The agency only provided advertising—nothing else was guaranteed. Plus, the whole setup was out of a cheap porn movie. There were five different escort agencies in one. They all had classy looking ads in the yellow pages promoting different names, complete with different numbers, but all the calls came to the same back room of a rundown house in a grungy part of town. If the owner had tried renting his house, the health authority would have shut him down, but while we girls sat around in the back he made more from our calls than he would have in rent. We would literally sit in this pig hole and take turns answering the phone for our turn on a call; the only thinking you had to do was to remember which line you were answering so you would quote the right agency name.

Two things brought this to a close for me. First, I turned eighteen and inherited far too much money. But what sent me over the edge was after having gone on a call, I was waiting in the fellow's hotel room for my cab to show up. He'd been decent enough—had even paid in American dollars—a trucker just passing through, so I sat and chatted with him while I waited for my cab. The agency called the room; I guess I'd been gone a little longer than they thought was okay, so they called to make sure things were on the up and up. Funny that they thought they were looking out for me—truly, had I been dead in the hotel room, all the phoning in the world wouldn't have changed things—and no, that never occurred to me either.

At any rate, when I got back to the agency they wanted double the fee since I had stayed with the client rather than in the lobby waiting for my taxi. That finished things for me. I tore a verbal strip off of the agency person, refused to pay, and left. Did they think I really needed them for this? Not a chance. Josie stayed on a while; she was a lot less hotheaded than I was.

I was in no major need of money, so I returned to our pizza place. I'd missed the fun and party atmosphere, and by now Roger had calmed down about our being underage. Plus, I'm sure he'd missed the incredible cash out we brought to the place. Josie eventually came back too; we always had more fun together. If we shopped, it was together; if we partied, it was together; if we decided to hitchhike to a lake to spend the day, it was together.

So there we were, back at the pizza place, but this time I had too much cash at hand. While I had done drugs off and on throughout the years, it had never been a driving force, just something I did to kill boredom. Now, with too much disposable cash, I was spending at least a hundred dollars a day. Not always the hard stuff; acid was as hard as I would go, but I noticed that with money you could certainly buy a much better grade of pot. I didn't realize then (nor did I care) that the reason we were getting such an incredible high and paying so much was that it must have been laced. Again, nothing to concern myself with.

Josie and I lived the high life. If I wanted to shop and Josie didn't have enough money, no problem; I would pay. I had money to burn. Whatever I wanted to do, Josie and I would do together. We went on like this for quite a while.

During this time, we would meet up with Henry for coffee or dinner or the like. I know he constantly prayed for me, and probably for her too. It's interesting how God can use something small to change the course of a life.

One time after meeting him, he simply said, "You guys are like hamsters going in circles on those wheels, but you never go anywhere. You're always going in circles to end up in the same place."

No big sermon, no preaching, just divinely timed words. We left dinner and went home shaking our heads. This didn't make sense. Our lives were exactly that—going nowhere and on the fast track getting there!

Well, as God would have it, my grandfather had a basement suite for rent. We had wanted it years earlier, but any time it came open we were content in our apartment. Then we'd always end up moving, and would regret not taking the basement suite. This time, although we had an amazing apartment and everything fine-tuned as far as our comings and goings, we decided it was time to take the plunge, to rent a place that we knew in our hearts would be a little more stable. We also knew that men coming and going just wasn't going to fly. In taking the basement suite, we were actually taking a baby step toward getting our lives together.

Henry was always praying. He never quit. Nor did he try to whitewash what he knew by now was a demonic problem. There was a speaker—Mike Warnke—who at the time was popular in Christian circles; he'd apparently been involved in the occult, and now had a powerful Christian testimony. Henry and Annie not only bought Josie and me tickets to see him, but also offered to babysit so we could go. While they helped substantially with Nadine—they were quick to buy clothes, toys, food, and so on—they were never quick to babysit. It was annoying then, but now I see the wisdom in them not enabling our lifestyle.

Anyway, we decided to go. The man was amazing! He not only put into words some of the terrors I had experienced in my own life, but he presented Jesus in a way that was actually inviting. He was quite funny, too, which only endeared him more to me. Well, Josie and I thought we might give this a shot. Deep down I already knew better, while for her it was a real first step.

Again, without deliverance (the eviction of my own demons, and who knows, perhaps my friend had some of her own by now), moving forward in a productive Christian lifestyle would be strained at best. We did attend church off and on, we did go to some women's meetings with Melody, my praying Christian landlady from years ago, but somehow we never quite connected. I believe we were "saved"; we did truly and fully accept Christ as our savior and we did want to live for Him. At the same time, though, we had not had deliverance. Can a Christian have a demon? I would say yes. In the same way a cancer-ridden person can accept Jesus but still have cancer, we were demon-ridden but had accepted Jesus.

Josie began working in offices again, and I continued waitressing, but took the odd course to try to break into the office world. I had since ended my relationship with Frank and was just on the prowl here and there.

I met a girl, Rebecca, in a class I was taking. We were casual friends. She had a boyfriend named Damien who seemed to have an interest in me. This was more my comfort zone—playing with the guy while befriending the girl. Not much of a Christian witness, to be sure, but then again I still had my dancing demons. I can't explain why I continued to see these two people. Really, they weren't my type, but there was still a strange draw. Rebecca offered to babysit one night, and I wasn't going to pass up free babysitting, so off Josie and I went.

When I went to pick up Nadine the next morning, something felt wrong, but I couldn't put my finger on it. They had Nadine, who was maybe three at the time, dressed in Rebecca's white silk housecoat. She did look cute, but something was off. I never let them babysit again, but did maintain my friendship with the two.

Rebecca and Damien did eventually break up, and Damien slowly crept into my world. He moved across the street into a basement suite directly facing ours.

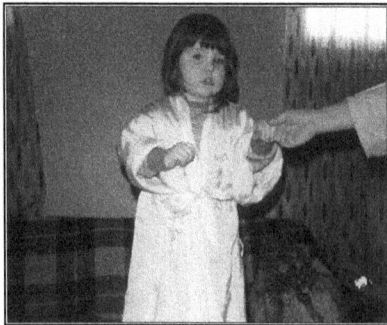

Something was off—Nadine was not her happy giggly self

Chapter Fourteen

Over the months Damien inserted himself into our lives as a really great friend and neighbor, while unknown to me he was also controlled by the same kind of demons, who were bent on destroying not only him but also me. We talked a lot, and it turned out he had an occult past too. This was a draw for me—he was someone who could relate to my stories.

The kicker came one day when I was recounting my story of the mysterious ride with the stranger who'd scared me in BC, and before I could finish my story, he turned to me and said, "You should have been playing with Barbies."

I almost jumped out of my skin! I had told no one to this point about that day. No one.

He went on to say, "You thought I was the devil."

Okay, now I was horrified, and yet drawn to him. How could he have known this?! What was the connection?

He went on to tell me that he'd been sent to grab me and take me to a satanic coven. He explained he was having a hard time because of where I was, surrounded by Bible-believing Christians who understood the demonic. He told me that on the day when I'd been invisibly attacked in the grass when I turned down the "wrong" road, the scratches were from him trying to grab hold of me, but he hadn't been able to because of the Christians and the power of their prayers.

If that wasn't enough to completely send my brain into never-never land, he went on to tell me how, many years ago, he'd lived in the same apartment as Josie and me, and had even had *a fern* in his bathroom! The night I couldn't remember—except for the fern—had been a demonic encounter of the worst kind.

Whether that was true, and it was actually him from years ago, or whether it was simply the demons telling him what had happened and what to say, I may never know, but the point is it intrigued me and actually drew me to him. Though this horrified me, I was truly drawn to the darkness of the past and the idea that we'd been intertwined in the intervening years. It also gave me an explanation for why, all those years ago, after waking up on the stairs all bruised up, I'd had the strangest desire for demonic sex.

For a little while, Damien was my boyfriend; although I was never quite committed to the idea, there was a pull there that I couldn't explain. He actually proposed—ring, flowers, and all. We decided on a certain night with a justice of the peace. I was waitressing split shifts at a certain restaurant, and when the night arrived when we were to get married, I was asked to work. Any normal person who was in love would have simply declined—but no, as divine intervention would have it, I called him to say, "Sorry we can't get married tonight—I have to work."

Damien was understandably annoyed—working a three-hour shift at a restaurant took priority over getting married? The next day something at the restaurant annoyed me, so I simply quit. Yes, I put off getting married to work in a restaurant that I would quit the next day.

God's spirit was working in me to prevent me from making yet another major blunder with my life. *Thank you, Henry, for all your praying!*

Some clarity managed to sink through my brain—marrying Damien wasn't something I truly wanted to do. This should have been obvious long before, but thankfully, God is patient and meets us where we are—he used the restaurant to get past the demons in my brain and insert some common sense.

I broke up with Damien. He didn't take it well, and he also didn't give up; he continued to live across the street and did his best to maintain a "friendship" with Josie and me. I'm beyond certain he was (and without Jesus, still is) even more demonically driven than I was.

One afternoon I came home from work with Nadine, having secured the dream waitressing job—Monday–Friday, 9 a.m.–5 p.m. (office hours in a restaurant setting!)—to a satanic pentagram painted in black paint across my entire kitchen floor! I grabbed Nadine and promptly headed back outside. I called Henry and asked him to please come over.

When he got there, I was still a little scared to venture into the house—I knew what an inverted pentagram meant and what it was for—but he went in without hesitation. He did something I thought was very unchristian. While he took the paint thinner and removed the symbol, he prayed that God would "return this curse to the head of the sender." I'd never heard of such a thing! A Christian sending a curse? It was one thing for it to just happen—as it had years ago in BC when I was on the other side—but to return a curse on purpose?

I seriously questioned Henry; was he playing with the occult too? Henry explained it was indeed biblical, as in Psalm 109 where David returns the curse to the head of the sender. I was a little too scared to argue, so okay, if this was indeed biblical, he could return it all he wanted as long as it wasn't on me or in my house. Henry left, and I managed to muster up enough bravery to return to my house.

Later that night, as I was sitting with a friend from the restaurant, a frantic knock came on my door. It was Damien. His forehead was split open, and blood was pulsing out at an alarming rate! My friend quickly left, and I called an ambulance. While we waited, Damien, visibly and understandably shaken, told me how he'd been just driving along and *bang!* It was like something had hit his head and split it open. After he left for the hospital, I called Henry to tell him of this strange happening.

What Henry said shook me to the core. "Well, given we returned the curse to sender, do you think Damien painted the pentagram?"

The picture became clear! With Damien's shock and confusion at something suddenly splitting his head open, and Henry's returning of the curse, and given my history with Damien—suddenly, yes, it all made sense! Damien was still a pawn in the occult world sent to work against me, and God in His mercy had spared me and shown me His incredible power.

I determined not to allow Damien into my house any longer and to seriously curtail my association with him. While a smart move on my end, what I should have done instead was to fall on my knees and cry out to God for deliverance and forgiveness and to get a right-living relationship going with Him. Instead I settled for just more knowledge *of* God, not a functioning relationship *with* God.

This started a new series of events in which the dark side played havoc in my world.

Chapter Fifteen

One sunny Saturday afternoon, Nadine was watching her favorite cartoons, and Josie and I went into the laundry room just beside the kitchen to finish up a week's worth of dirty laundry. Suddenly, Nadine was screaming at the top of her lungs. We lunged the three feet back to see Nadine covered in little bugs, which were also lining the kitchen floor and walls. Incredible! We had been gone forty-five seconds, and suddenly my daughter was covered in these bugs, as was the kitchen.

Josie grabbed a broom and started sweeping the insects off of Nadine, while I grabbed the phone and called Henry. She managed to get the bugs off, and we ran outside to wait for Henry. We weren't brave enough to go back into our suite until he arrived. No bugs! Not a trace of them—nothing. As with the black panther from years gone by, there was no trace of the horror.

The only thing that kept me from thinking I'd completely lost my mind was that this time both Nadine and Josie had seen and experienced it—I wasn't imagining things; it had been real. Josie and I both knew deep down that it was demonic, but we kept those thoughts to ourselves. Saying it out loud would only make it more real; better to believe that a bunch of bugs had suddenly gotten into the house because it was a warm day, and just as suddenly, they were gone—they must have flown out down the drain... Yeah, that sounded much better.

If this had been the only occurrence, we could have probably stayed in our blissful state of denial. Days or weeks later—I can't truly say—we were lying in bed. We still shared a king-size bed, while Nadine had her own room. We were awake and chatting, and without warning the clothes in the closet started moving as if someone was brushing by them— yet not a window in the place was open. This in itself was strange, but days later we were doing laundry and the very clothes that had been swaying in the nonexistent wind came out of the washer with large tears in them. They looked like three large claws had ripped right through them. This was especially strange and upsetting, as it happened to two of our identical dresses. (We frequently bought the same items and would wear them out partying).

We tried to rationalize it, convincing ourselves that something in the washing machine must have ripped them, yet deep down we knew differently.

Before the next load, we double-checked the washer: nothing sharp. We put the load in and literally sat on the washing machine while it went through the cycles. The clothes were fine, so we put them in the dryer; to our dismay, our other identical outfits came out with identical clawlike rips yet again—and there was nothing at all in the dryer to explain this. Unsettling, to say the least.

Another night—while we were sleeping—Nadine came into our room and said something had woken her and scared her. Not yet at the place where I would venture to pray against anything—I remembered the night in the apartment, and yet I still wasn't walking right with God—I told Nadine, "You have a guardian angel from God—take his hand and he'll go to your room with you." I said more to make her feel better, yet I still fully expected her to pop into bed with Josie and me.

What happened next was amazing; Nadine turned her head to look up at something unseen and reached up with her hand as if she was holding hands with someone. Then she turned to us, said "Okay," and went to bed.

Neither Josie nor I slept for a while that night. What had Nadine seen? Why didn't we see the angel? What had just happened? I even went to her room to see if I could see anything, but there she was, alone and peacefully asleep again.

Chapter Sixteen

And so it went on, like a mini house of horrors. This may have been why Josie decided it was time to move. Not far, mind you—we were, after all, still best friends—she simply moved up the block to an apartment by herself. But physically moving to distance herself from a spiritual problem didn't help; because we were both so bound up with demons, some moved with her and some stayed at my house.

When she first moved, she complained about crazy nightmares—totally demonic dreams that left her terrified. The demonic revealed just how strong its hold on us was when physical manifestations started to happen.

We both had photo albums that kept a log of our "party" days—soft-porn pictures, if you will. One day I noticed mine was gone, so I called Josie to see if she remembered where I had left it. She was most shocked to find it at her apartment. Okay, we could excuse this—she took it by mistake, and she would return it. Before we got together again, however, the album showed up back at my house. I called her to thank her, assuming she must have dropped it off while I was out, but to our dismay she said she hadn't returned it. When it showed up at her house again days later, we were fully convinced something was wrong. Again, this might have been a good time to fall on my knees and call out for God's deliverance, mercy, and love, but with the demonic spiritual blinders we both had on, we chose a different solution.

Josie threw out the photo album in the dumpster behind her apartment. Of course, it reappeared again. Other things started coming and going; I recall looking for a hammer one day, only to find it the next morning in front of my door.

Time marched on, with strange happenings now becoming more normal in our lives. At some point we both decided that our current jobs weren't enough, so we decided to head back to school. We were both accepted, and she decided to move back to Bonnyville, where she was originally from, to work and save money till school started. While I did start school, she stayed back home a while longer and never did join me. She eventually moved back to Edmonton and got married. While we stayed in touch during this period, we started to drift; she had her world that was relatively normal, and I had mine.

This was an interesting strategy that the dark side again used—she got married, and was living a status quo life, so the dark side turned down its activity. If she assumed that life was good and normal (without the true power of God), she would not feel the need to turn to Him. The same could be said for me; I went to school, passed courses, and things stopped going bump in the night.

While in school I met new friends: not Christian but not occult-involved, so I settled for the "normal" life. I would go out to nightclubs on Friday and Saturday, started going to church on Sundays, and would study and attend school during the week. From the outside, things appeared to be right on track for a life in this world.

Chapter Seventeen

At this point I had a new roommate, Collette, who I'd met at church. She was a sold-out believer, while I was still playing "church" with God, but God used her in an incredible way! Even though I was going to church, I still had an insatiable craving for sex, and still the dark kind—church on Sunday, school during the week, and demonic sex on the weekend, back to church Sunday, rinse and repeat. Yes, I was just like a lot of so-called Christians who go to church on Sunday and live like hell the rest of the week.

One night I had a dream.

I was at home in the basement getting rid of pesky critters that were coming in the house. I was shooing them out and slamming the door on them. Suddenly, there was a *bang* upstairs, and I realized I hadn't locked the front door. I ran up to see what was going on. When I got upstairs, there was a large man with a wire in his hand. I ran to the side door where two moving men (*big* men) were carrying furniture in; they attempted to stop the man with the wire, but somehow he overpowered them and followed me downstairs. His intention was to rape and kill me by strangling me while slicing my neck...

I woke up! Now fully awake and in a total sweat, I got up to go to Collette's room; I was terrified and needed physical company. As I got up, I was gently—very gently—pushed back. Okay, back to horrified, and yet, the push back was like nothing I had ever experienced in my occult days—it was truly gentle. All of a sudden (and yes, I was fully awake! And again, not stoned) a black tarlike substance started flowing out of my chest up to the ceiling; it was like tar and elastic all at the same time. There was a final vigorous pull, and it snapped right out of me and out of the ceiling and was gone. It was only then that I could get to my feet.

I ran so fast to Collette's room that I'm sure I went faster than the speed of light. I thought I'd have to wake her up, but instead, she was sitting up and said to me, "Hey, what's going on? God woke me up a while ago and told me to pray for you. I've been praying and praying! What's happening?"

If my head wasn't already spinning, now it was doing cartwheels too. I began to tell her about my dream, and as I spoke the dream aloud the interpretation unfolded and came clearer with every single word.

The critters in the basement that I was shooing out and then locking the door on were the obvious sins in my life. I had thrown out occult jewelry, pictures, and even all of the clothes I associated, even remotely, with anything occult. I wasn't openly practicing the occult—I got rid of and closed the door on everything obvious. What I had overlooked was the state of my heart, and the demonic stronghold from years ago (the demonic sex that I still participated in) symbolized by the strong man at the front door that I had forgotten about. The two moving men were my conscience; all the while I was participating in my sexual exploits, I knew deep down it was wrong but couldn't stop. This is why, as big and powerful as they were, they couldn't stop the intruder that I had long ago let in. My lifestyle would kill me.

At the moment I fully understood my dream, I also re-alized that the elastic tar that was removed from me was the work of God. He performed deliverance on me that very night. That also explained the very gentle push back while the tar was being removed.

Don't go getting your theological knickers in a knot—God cannot and will not be boxed. While folks associate deliverance with screaming and frothing, that's not always the case. God will do as He pleases. Is this any stranger than healing a blind man by spitting in the mud rather than just praying? I had been asking God to get rid of this ugly desire, and He answered—His way.

I cried and cried as I realized what had just happened. Collette was happy to finally know why God had interrupted her sleep to pray; she was obedient and had prayed for hours without knowing why. Between her prayers and God's amazing grace and mercy on me that night, I was finally free.

With her no-nonsense attitude, Collette then said to me, "Okay, now I know why I had to pray. You're free. I'd like to go to sleep now, if God will let me."

I went back to bed and had the most peaceful sleep. I also stopped playing church; I renewed my personal relationship with Christ and attended church to hear and learn, not just to put in my time. Christ was now my Savior, Lord, and best friend. I finally had true happiness, I had real peace, and I was truly loved and forgiven. Life was amazing!

The end?

In a perfect world this would be the end, and we would all live happily ever after. But this wasn't the case. The forces of darkness will not give up; while they do need to ask God's permission before doing anything, their mission is still to destroy—and if they couldn't take me to hell, well, they would at least do their very best to interfere with my victorious Christian life.

Chapter Eighteen

Having been set free of my crazy demonic desires and now enjoying a real, living relationship with Jesus, I was faced with a new problem.

During the time I'd been living with Collette and playing church, I had also been seriously dating a DJ from a local club that my friend and I frequented. He spun records not only in the club where we danced but also at the strip club that was attached. Edward wasn't a bad person, just not saved; he lived the same empty life most humans accept as normal. He had a regular job during the week, and supplemented his income on the weekends working in the club.

Well, I knew that God wasn't big on dating nonbelievers, so rather than just end the relationship I decided to do what so many people do today—I would "missionary date." I told Edward of my relationship with Christ and invited him to church. He came willingly and often. I had decided in my own head that if he didn't accept Christ within a certain amount of time, I would in fact end the relationship. In the meantime, I had also told him that sex was off the table. Because he knew of my past, I had put it to him this way: "I'm the most expensive whore on the block. My prices are in line with what Jesus thinks of me. I now charge a lifetime commitment for sex, and you have to prequalify to purchase."

I was never one to hide from my past, and was actually quite open about it; my thinking was, "If I'm upfront I can never get blackmailed." I had known too many people with secrets that could seriously damage them. I also reasoned that if the God of this universe knew all about it and had forgiven me, what did I care what humans thought? I've always been able to relate to the story of Rahab in Joshua 2. She was a prostitute who turned to God, and throughout the Bible she's known as "the prostitute who God saved," so I figured I was in good company.

Well, Edward attended church and apparently listened; one day I got a phone call from him. "I think I need to quit the club, especially the strip club. I don't think it's right."

I was over-the-moon happy—my "missionary dating" seemed to have paid off.

Not only was I playing with fire with my missionary dating, but Edward and I were actually living together at the time. While sex may have been off the table, we were still playing house, so we reasoned the right thing to do was to get married.

We got married and lived happily ever after. The end, right? No!

We had many good times and many ups and downs as well. My daughter was now in grade school, I was working steady, Edward was working steady, and we attended church together, so by all appearances things were great.

We had one big issue: sex. I had been waiting a very long time for "guilt-free sex," the kind that was okay by God, but on our wedding night Edward had a little too much wine and actually called me names like "slut" and "whore." I never truly forgave him or got over it, so for the duration of our marriage I was seldom interested in sex, which did cause a lot of strain on our marriage. When God says to forgive each other daily and not to *"give the devil a foothold"* by *"let[ting] the sun go down while you are still angry"* (Ephesians 4:26–27), He isn't strongly suggesting it, He's ordering it for our own good. Although Edward was in no way perfect, I will say that the hurt I harbored and my inability to forgive in a large part led to marriage destruction in the ensuing years.

My wedding day

My friend Collette had moved out a while back. We'd still been living together when Edward had moved in. Her stance was, "I don't agree with what you're doing; you can't live together and not be married, so he goes or I go." Obviously, it was she who left. To be clear, I can absolutely respect that stance: she was never mean or cruel or judgmental; she just commendably made her stand.

What is tragic is that much later on she would end up living with a fellow, have kids, and never get married; she would excuse it by saying, "In the eyes of God, we're married." Seriously? Yet it's a common situation with Christians even today—people often excuse away what God says if it inconveniences them. I know this to have been true in my own life, and I see it far too often in the world today.

Nonetheless, long before her later, more compromised Christianity, she was attending a church and seeing a youth pastor. She said she'd talked to him and mentioned my involvement in the occult. Would I come talk to the group about how it operated and give my story?

Sure I would! Finally some redeeming purpose for the crap in my life; maybe I could make a difference to somebody else.

Off I went on the Sunday we'd arranged. I was actually so nervous I could barely talk—me, the big talker, sweating it out in a room full of teenagers who all wanted to hear what I had to say.

I talked for a bit but was still nervous, so I prayed silently: "God, what do I say?"

What I asked next was, "Has anyone here taken a drama class and been asked to visualize their spirit guide and talk with it?"

I almost fell over when ninety percent of the hands in the room went up. *What was this?* An entire generation being taught the occult practice of summoning a demon under the pleasant guise of "visualizing their guide." Well, this was where I knew for sure what to talk about. I discussed with the room how things really boil down to two spiritual entities—good (angels, or the Godhead: God the father, God the son, Jesus, and God the Holy Spirit) or bad (demons and Satan). I explained there's no in-between, and what they were actually doing was summoning a demon to be their personal guide.

All a demon needs is an invitation. Leviticus 19:31 says, *"Do not turn to mediums or seek out spiritists, for you will be defiled by them. I am the Lord your God."* The invitation can even be unknowing. Hosea 4:6 says, *"...my people are destroyed from lack of knowledge."*

Here I had a roomful of kids who had unknowingly invited a demonic presence into their lives. The discussion turned into a Holy Spirit-energized talk about truth and the exposing of lies and the "how to" of combating the enemy.

Our time came to an end far too quickly; at the end I had a lineup of teenagers who wanted to ask specific questions or tell me their issues. There were too many, so instead of keeping them there for hours, I yelled out for everyone to grab a pen and gave out my home number. I had no idea what this would start.

Over the next few weeks I would find myself on the phone nonstop with various kids. There were a couple in particular who seemed to have a real demonic problem, but also a hunger for truth. I asked them if they would like to do a Bible study. To my surprise, not only did they say yes, but they asked for it to be on a Friday night. A Friday night? Teenagers? These kids were hungry for truth.

Chapter Nineteen

With our own car, Edward and I would pick up the kids on Friday nights for an informal Bible study. Anything went. No question, no topic, was taboo, and if we didn't have the answers right away, we'd all dive into the Bible and do research together. Then they started asking about inviting friends; before too long we'd be picking up teenagers in different trips (they wouldn't all fit in the one car), and we'd sometimes be at it till one a.m., at which point we'd drive them home.

The kids got closer with each other and God. We didn't tell them what church to go to, only that they should find a Bible-believing church in their neighborhood. But in the meantime, the Friday meetings grew and grew.

My daughter was younger at the time, so sometimes she'd stick around; other times she'd head off to her room to play. Most of the kids were a bit older than her, but they all seemed to want to include her in everything. We had a large Christmas dinner for those attending, and we'd put on barbecues from time to time. Some came to our church with us and were baptized there, while others simply wanted to get baptized with their own group, so Edward and I actually baptized a few (at their request) in our own bathtub, with the Bible study kids all crammed into our tiny bathroom to witness this.

Some days it felt like the church of the Bible—no religion, just believers gathered to worship. Since Edward had been a DJ, he would put together mix tapes of praise and worship; we'd photocopy the words and hand them out. Because we weren't exactly equipped with musical instruments, we'd play the tapes loud on the stereo and sing along as if there was an actual worship team. The worship time became more and more amazing—sometimes lasting hours. At times, one or more would start crying and be in their own world with the Lord; other times, Holy Spirit joy would flood the place and laughter would break out.

Kids came and went. We had one set of girls from a group home, and to this day I can't recall who invited them or how they came to be there (although God knows). Driving them home one night, I heard the most profound thing. One girl said to the other, "I know it's wrong, but I don't want to be a virgin anymore. I'm like the only one. I just want to lose my virginity." I had something to say to that, but God shut me up and instead, the other girl said, "You can lose your virginity any day; at any time you can become a non-virgin. But I can never, ever be a virgin again. I wish I was you instead."

Wow! Talk about God's wisdom coming out. The other girl paid attention. God used the teenagers to speak to each other. It was amazing.

We also did deliverance—not frequently, but on occasion. Outside of the Bible study group, a few people came privately knowing they had a problem, and we would tackle that too; God was rocking in our house. For Nadine, it got to a point where demons manifesting or people "drunk" in the Holy Spirit was nothing unusual—for her it was the norm.

We had a new attendee, Rick, who was involved in the occult. Again, I can only sum up his presence there as a "God invitation," as I don't recall him having a connection with anyone there. He was truly caught in a demonic web; it was clear he wanted freedom, but something would always interrupt him before he took the final step. We wouldn't push deliverance on him, as the Bible is clear that a person has to want freedom and Jesus. We would have done him a disservice expelling his demons if he didn't then turn it all to Jesus; they would have simply returned and made him worse off. As Matthew 12:43–45 says,

> When an impure spirit comes out of a person, it goes through arid places seeking rest and does not find it. Then it says, "I will return to the house I left." When it arrives, it finds the house unoccupied, swept clean and put in order. Then it goes and takes with it seven other spirits more wicked than itself, and they go in and live there. And the final condition of that person is worse than the first. That is how it will be with this wicked generation.

One night Rick called, yelling and swearing and threatening to come over and kill Edward. Edward invited him over. Now, while we both knew this was merely demonic talk, we still called my parents to pray while Rick and his demons were on the way over. My praying parents showed up, and so did Rick—in his full demonic fury.

My parents and daughter were in the kitchen, praying and watching things unfold, when all of a sudden Rick stopped and looked around the room, his expression full of terror. When we asked what was wrong, he replied, "Don't you see them? There are angels everywhere."

Praise God! We didn't see them, but clearly something in Rick did; he did an about-face and left in a hurry.

I will admit that even though I knew God was bigger, stronger, and in control, I was still a little nervous having this large fellow in our living room full of murderous demons—well, until the demons themselves freaked out at "all the angels in the room." We sat around talking about this for quite a while afterward—a room full of big angels that we couldn't see, but that Rick had seen. How powerful!

This wasn't the end of Rick, but it's worth mentioning that at another point within this time period my husband said he wanted us to pray for deliverance for him (Edward, that is) "just to be sure." Why not? Folks go to the doctor for a physical when nothing is ailing them, so why not a spiritual checkup?

I asked my parents to deal with this, as I was too close and emotionally tied to Edward to want to handle anything that might have arisen. At the time, we had recently adopted a cat named Pye—a beautiful creature, with long beautiful fur and a regal bearing. Unfortunately, this cat would sometimes attack for no reason. He'd attached himself to my daughter's face one day and drawn blood. He'd also done this to me. We were on the verge of taking him back due to his erratic disposition, but God works in weird ways...

When my parents came to pray for Edward, he was on the couch with the cat perched beside him. My parents started praying for any spirits to come forth, and the cat got a serious hairball. We stopped praying because the cat was doing that cat thing, coughing up a hairball very loudly. Okay, when the cat was done, they picked up where they'd left off. Again, the cat loudly coughed up a hairball. This happened a couple times before my dad laughed and said, "I think the cat needs deliverance, not you!"

We prayed for any familiar spirits in the cat to be bound and removed. A few loud coughing fits and hairballs later, and Pye was a new cat. He jumped and cuddled my daughter and purred; he was all over everyone, as friendly as could be—no biting, no clawing, just all of a sudden a happy, friendly cat. The demons left, and the cat stayed.

As funny and cuddly as the evening was, it brings to light yet another Bible truth about "familiar objects": God warned His people over and over again to destroy idols, to destroy the plunder from the people they conquered. Why? Because He didn't want them to have the spoils of war? No! Because God allows demons (still under His control) to attach themselves to things, and He was trying to spare His people the demonic activity they would bring into their tents and their lands by keeping the cursed objects.

I was reminded that night that even innocent things (a beautiful cat, for instance) could have an occult history; perhaps its previous owner had been practicing the occult. Who knows? But God reminded me that night to pray over things I would bring in and to avoid questionable things. Deuteronomy 7:26 says, *"Do not bring a detestable thing into your house or you, like it, will be set apart for destruction."*

This sweet demon-possessed cat was certainly trying to destroy us—what lived in him did not like the one who was living in us. But in His mercy and wisdom, God used Edward's "spiritual checkup" to shed light on something else evil. God dealt with it, and we not only learned from it but had the friendliest, happiest, cuddliest cat for years to come.

Chapter Twenty

As far as Rick and generational curses go, some history is required here. I had known all my life I was adopted, but when I was with Edward, I got curious about things like "Why do I have brown hair?" and "Why is my nose so big?" So I decided to look up the biological side of things.

Records then were more open than in the past, so it wasn't difficult to find Eleanor, the woman who'd physically given birth to me. She had family in Edmonton, making it easy for her to come up and meet me.

We first met at a restaurant, then later she invited me to her sister's place to meet the family. I suppose after all those years, they were all curious. They were all nice enough people. When I got Eleanor alone, though, I had many questions about her and her life, and what I found out explained a lot! First, I found out that she'd gotten pregnant while having an affair with a married man—okay, generationally speaking, this could explain some of my own past.

Then I found out her father had not only had an affair himself, but that there had been abuse by him within the family. Now I understood the demonic influences in my life a whole lot better. The icing came when she told me her mother had been involved in "white witchcraft" and séances. Well, I got more answers than I'd bargained for about my history—the hair and nose didn't matter anymore! Now I fully understood how I could be so demonically screwed up from such a young age while growing up in a Christian home. Make no mistake—God doesn't play games. When He says in Deuteronomy 5:9 that *"You shall not bow down to them or worship them; for I, the Lord your God, am a jealous God, punishing the children for the sin of the parents to the third and fourth generation of those who hate me,"* He means it. All that Eleanor told me brought my life into a new context and made all those Bible verses about this sort of stuff even more relevant.

Through my biological mother, I also met a cousin, Dawn. Eleanor told me that I should meet her because she needed some stability in her life, but she had just one request: "Don't push your God stuff." I almost laughed out loud; my "God stuff" was the only thing that was going to help anyone!

To make a long story shorter, I met Dawn, and Edward and I adopted her. Not that she was especially young, but she was still underage, and her mother (Eleanor's sister) was heavily involved in the New Age and wasn't in favor of all this. We had to adopt her simply to get her some identification so she could exist as a legal person. She lived with us, was like a big sister to Nadine, attended and graduated a marketing college, and did come to accept Christ as her savior. I would also find out that Rick was a distant cousin of Dawn's; yes, biologically and spiritually speaking, this made him some sort of cousin of mine too. The demonic bloodline that ran through this family was amazing.

At any rate, life continued. My daughter was getting older and more and more versed in the supernatural, something she considered normal. And yet, with all this knowledge, something managed to escape all of us.

One day, after Nadine had gone on a school field trip, I got a call from the school. It turned out that my daughter, with all her head knowledge about God and the supernatural, with all her attending church and even going to a Christian school, had decided to attempt suicide on the field trip.

No, God didn't allow her to succeed, but it should have raised enough questions within me to make me look deeper into the demonic in her life (generational curses anyone?); instead, in my blindness I sent her for counseling and spent too much time talking with her instead of praying for her. Why would a kid who had it all, was spoiled beyond belief, enjoyed lots of friends, and knew God (or at least *about* Him) attempt suicide on a Christian school field trip? Any of this sounding familiar? It's amazing how stupid we can be! Here I was, having escaped an occult background, having helped teenagers from all over deal with it, yet I had failed to deal directly with it with my own daughter. This would come back to haunt us both later on in life.

In the meantime, things heated up with the Bible study group. Rick and three of his friends had committed a murder one night. Now, imagine that your teenage kids are going to a Bible study where a confessed murderer is attending. In a perfect world, one would say, "Praise God, he's attending!" but let's be real—even as Christians, our first reaction is to protect our children from the world. No, ideally, and biblically speaking, we're supposed to welcome all and believe that what is in us (and our kids) will be good influences.

Again, that's often not how we act. Why did I send my own daughter to a Christian school? To save her from the influences of the world. So, imagine nonbelieving parents hearing that their teenagers are attending a Bible study where a confessed murderer is on the loose and attending off and on. The Bible study quickly dwindled to only those over twenty who were free to choose to attend on their own.

Rick called us one night in a panic—could he come over? Well, of course he could. We also called a pastor friend well versed in deliverance, just in case. Rick arrived and was all over the map; he was a bundle of nerves. We'd already heard from the kids about what had happened, but we waited for him to tell us. He finally did and asked what he should do next; his first completely understandable inclination was to run far and fast.

Our pastor friend talked with him about Jesus and asked if he truly wanted to be free of all his terror. They prayed at length, and afterward the pastor said, "You know you have to do the right thing."

No one was going to force him to turn himself in, although we would have been obligated to call the police if Rick had decided to run. The choice was up to him. Rick sadly understood what this would mean, so his next question was, "What do we do next?"

The pastor said something that I'll never forget. "We order pizza, we eat pizza, then we take you to the police station. It'll be a long time before you have pizza again, so let's do that first."

This wasn't exactly what I had expected to hear, but order pizza we did. We sat and talked, ate, and prayed for a few hours, then Edward and the pastor drove Rick to the police station. In the end, after a lengthy well-publicized trial, he was convicted and sentenced to ten years—unfortunately, his friends didn't also get convicted.

Now try explaining *this* at work (I was relatively new at my job at the time): "I won't be in today—a kid from our Bible study murdered someone, so I have to go to court." I never had to think about how to tell folks at work that I was a believer—the trial did this for me within the first few weeks of my new employment.

Chapter Twenty-One

Time marched on—work, church, a much smaller Bible study, and my daughter. Yes, my daughter who was now turning toward the darkness. It wasn't an overnight change—had it been that obvious, perhaps I may have been smarter—but it was a very gradual shift from how she dressed, to the music she listened to, to the books she read, to her whole attitude about church and God. By the time I got my head out of my butt and realized just how demonized she was, the transformation had happened. She'd gone from going to youth group to partying on Friday nights; she'd gone from friendly and chatty to locking herself in her room.

Praying for her deliverance had most certainly crossed my mind, but there were two issues stopping me: first, she was my daughter and a little too close to home to pray for (or so I thought); and second, what if she didn't turn it around and come back to God? Then she'd end up even worse. In hindsight, I should have taken the chance on both, but my fear (note: *fear is not of God!*), the fear that she'd end up worse off, prevented me from initiating direct spiritual warfare on her behalf.

What we did instead was to frequently anoint the house—doors, windows, everything—and ask that God put angels on guard. Interestingly enough, Nadine was becoming more and more agitated while she was at home. Prayer does work.

One night in particular, God used my daughter to show a friend of mine the true existence of the demonic. Trixie had been attending Bible study for a few years, and she was one of the attendees old enough to have her own place. Make no mistake, she was a sold-out praying Christian, straight from a Bible-believing home. She knew Jesus!

Like many Christians today, however, she didn't believe—or perhaps wouldn't believe—in the direct power of the demonic and its hold on people. While we agreed on salvation, the power of prayer, and all the basics, she was of the mind that there was too much emphasis on the demonic, and it really wasn't as big a deal as we were making it out to be. Don't misunderstand—we all got along and were of one mind praying for people; it was just one of those things that she felt should not be focused on.

That night we'd all done our worship and study, and the Holy Spirit prompted us to anoint a little further. Even Trixie was agreeable to anointing; she did believe that God's anointing represented His power and presence.

Everyone knew Nadine had problems, so we concentrated on her room. We specifically anointed her door, her TV, her phone, and her bed. When Nadine came home that night, she was the regular Nadine—she said hi to everyone and went to her room. Nanoseconds later, she came out with a demonic look of fury, and she was screaming and yelling expletives at me, telling me to take her phone, TV, bed, and door—it wasn't lost on anybody that she was only cursing at the very things we had anointed. Then she stormed back to the room.

I was used to this "switching" between the demons and my daughter, so it wasn't much of a shock to me, but to the others—Trixie in particular—it was an eye-opener. I quietly prayed that God would bind the demons in Nadine and shut them up, and allow Nadine to be Nadine.

A few minutes later, Nadine came out of her room normal, seemingly unaware of her previous outburst. She came into the living room and said, "So... when did you guys get here? Whatcha up to?" Perfectly normal. Trixie made a relatively fast exit that night, but I believe that God used this incident to teach her the reality of the demonic.

We all still met and prayed on a regular basis, and Nadine's manifesting became the norm. Again, I wish I'd prayed for deliverance rather than just binding the demons every time they showed up, but I always feared making things worse. Yes, even as a functioning Christian aware of the devil and his schemes, I still managed to be blinded by them. Let's be honest here—I'm not perfect; to this day I can get caught with my guard down and walk head on into situations I need to ask God to forgive me for. Being a Christian doesn't mean I'm perfect—just forgiven and loved.

In time, I learned that Nadine was not only skipping school but not even attending. Besides delving into the occult, she had begun cutting herself on a regular basis—another demonic trait. As it says in 1 Kings 18:28, *"So they shouted louder and slashed themselves with swords and spears, as was their custom, until their blood flowed."*

How many times do I need to mention generational curses? Yes, while the Bible speaks of generational blessings for those who love God, until the curses are dealt with—well... Nadine was turning into a mini-me from years gone by. My heart was breaking into a million pieces on a daily basis.

Then came the day that God started showing me things. I had been feeling an urgency at work to go home. I shrugged it off for a while, but the feeling only got stronger, so I finally left. I came home from work and Nadine's room was a mess— nothing unusual at all about this. While looking at the mess supernaturally, though, I knew that Nadine had come home and lost her virginity. I know it was God who told me.

I called Nadine on her cell and told her that she needed to come home right away. When she arrived, I said, "So, you lost your virginity today, eh?"

She was indignant. "How did you know?" she screamed.

I didn't quite have an answer to that, so I said, "Your bed was a mess."

She laughed. "My bed is *always* a mess. How did you know?"

The only real answer I could give was, "God told on you, so I could pray."

Turns out I had missed her and the boy by minutes; had I acted a little faster on the urgency I felt at work, things may have been halted for the time. When God tells you to do something, *do it*! Don't wait.

During this demonic onslaught our family was facing, Toronto, Canada was experiencing revival. There was a little airport church that God had decided to visit. This church was making the news for its antics—people roaring like lions, falling over and crying or laughing. From the outside it sounded absolutely bizarre and crazy, yet God is never one to be put in a box. My parents weren't ones to have the media make up their mind, so they announced one day, "We're all going to the Toronto church. If it's God, we don't want to miss it; if it's not, we'll know for ourselves."

Imagine if we all lived this way—finding out truth for ourselves instead of being fed and believing whatever the media or even churches sometimes throw out. Edward and I were quite excited to be able to go. In the evening, we went to tell Nadine the good news. What we walked into was pure demonic manifestation.

"Nadine, guess what?"

She glared and growled. "We're going to that stupid church, aren't we? I don't want to go!"

This was so similar to what had happened to me years ago in BC, where something in me "knew"—and now something in Nadine "knew"—that we were going to this church, and it certainly didn't want to go. After seeing her reaction, I was fairly convinced this church must be doing a God thing—demons don't get upset when people are fake and just playing church. I was pretty excited, thinking that Nadine might get the deliverance she needed.

The flight there was smooth—Nadine was Nadine, and most of the time she seemed excited to be flying somewhere, going to a hotel, and eating out for the weekend; the other times when she would "switch" and manifest, she was angry and miserable about the prospect.

We got settled in our hotel and made our way to the church. This was where things got interesting. Getting into the church was difficult—Nadine was angry, then not feeling well (how I remembered this from my BC encounter), and she spent some time in the bathroom before being dragged into the service.

During the worship that was so electric with God's presence, Nadine was beyond angry—hate was oozing out of her every pore. God's presence was very real and powerfully felt, invading the place, and so was the hate emanating from Nadine. My heart was breaking again—here I was encountering God in such a powerful way, feeling His love, His grace, and yet beside me was a shell of my daughter overtaken by evil. I felt not only powerless against it (which in reality I wasn't), but guilty that I should be enjoying God while I could see she was suffering.

Nadine and I were sitting away from my family, who were in the middle of everything, while I could only manage to drag

Nadine near to the back of the auditorium. We were seated in a long row. There was an elderly lady near the end closest to the aisle, a few empty seats, then Nadine, and me beside her. The preaching started, and we were all seated. All of a sudden, from a sitting position, Nadine leapt up, cleared the empty seats and the elderly lady, hit the aisle, and ran full force out of the building.

It took a couple seconds to get over the shock of what I'd just seen. Nadine had moved like a cat, literally pouncing from a seated position, clearing four chairs, and hitting the ground running. The little elderly lady turned to my shocked face, and said, "Oh, demons, eh?"

Ya *think*?

I made my way out of the place to find Nadine sitting outside in a corner, crying.

She said, "Mom, do you think I actually have demons? I'm beginning to think I might."

Okay, I'd just watched hate ooze out of her, I'd watched her perform an impossible physical feat—and she was saying she *might* have demons.

I burst out laughing! The situation was so serious, so bizarre, so demonic, and all I could do was laugh?

She and I talked at length outside the church about the reality of the situation. Just like way back in my demon-infested apartment, had we followed through on deliverance things may have gone differently, but in my spiritual stupor I just sat back and waited for God to do His thing—never once thinking that maybe this wasn't a spectator sport but rather, participation was required.

God had also tried to warn me and show me something while at this church. I had a "vision": it was Nadine, and out of her were coming these snakes, large and thick. God took them and tied them in a knot so they were writhing and smashing about until they suffocated. The snakes died, but there was a nest inside with unhatched eggs. When I say Christians can be stupid, I'm also talking about myself. The eggs! I needed to deal with the eggs! Did I? *No!*

Nadine's demons got smart—they hid quietly for the next day. I'm sure they were uncomfortable and tormented (this gives me a degree of satisfaction), but Nadine maintained a show of "normal," so we headed back home and I prayed things would be fine.

Fine was not what happened next; a new demonic chapter was unfolding.

A little while later, Edward and I found Nadine stuffing her belongings into a duffel bag. When we asked what she was doing, she brazenly announced she'd had enough and was running away. I recalled that when I was younger and demonically driven, I'd also felt the need to run away from a home that was Christian, filled with the Holy Spirit, and aware of the demonic. I didn't argue with her, as I knew from my own life there was no stopping her. I could temporarily detain her, but determined as she was, she'd go anyway. So we just did what any normal parents (okay, normal in our world) would do: we said we'd give her and her duffel bag a ride wherever she planned to go. The only source of amusement in this whole scene was the shocked and confused look on her face when we offered her the ride so she wouldn't have to lug this huge bag with her, rather than trying to stop her. She asked us to drop her off at school, which we did that morning.

I went to work broken. How Edward managed at work, I don't know, but as for me, my heart was beyond fractured. I did my best to focus at work and remind myself that God was in control, all while trying to answer the phone, remain composed, and do my regular work.

As God would have it, I had a job that was not only union but very understanding. Someone told me to take stress leave. What? Christians don't take stress leave—they rely fully on God. Is stress leave okay for a Christian? I wrestled with this. In the end, I did manage about a month off work, which to me seemed like admitting defeat, but God used the time to build me back up and get me ready for battle.

I found myself praying at length—daytime, nighttime, in the bathroom, at the fridge. My time with God was the only thing that kept me from a complete breakdown. During this time, God reminded me about spiritual warfare—something I should have been thinking about the entire time, instead of wallowing in the fear and hurt for my daughter. Yes, God is beyond patient and understanding, and unlike a lot of Christians running around, God doesn't shoot His wounded—He picks them up, dusts them off, and says, "Let's do this right this time."

I started walking around the area that was popular with the runaways of the day. I would go and quietly pray (demons aren't deaf, no need to scream); I would pray for God to smash the teeth of the demonic, to release angels with fiery swords dipped in the Blood of Jesus and slice those demons into pieces, to release all the prisoners and yes, even to cause the demons more pain than they were causing me. I was beyond angry, but I believe it was a righteous anger. My parents would come from time to time and do the same, as would my husband. If Satan was going to try to take my kid, I was gonna stand with God and rob Satan of all the other kids he was deceiving.

I believe this is a type of revenge God allows—righteous revenge, I called it. One cold winter night, there was my daughter, passed out drunker than a skunk on the sidewalk. Righteous anger or not, knowing God was ultimately in control didn't stop the tears that flowed as I stepped over her, prayed for her, and continued the prayer walk. God had already told me not to bring her home, that she would have to come back on her own when He arranged it. I prayed especially hard that she wouldn't find shelter in a dumpster, drunk and passed out, and find herself in eternity after being compacted with the garbage collection.

Over and over, my bottom-line prayer for her was "Don't allow her to step into eternity without You—keep her alive to be two hundred years old if need be."

Just because something is God's will doesn't guarantee smooth sailing or freedom from doubt—ask the disciples in the boat crossing the sea. Jesus told them to go—he was right there with them—yet a storm came that still caused anxiety.

My family and I would go out on prayer walks and quietly pray for the kids on the street and the whole area in general. One day the Holy Spirit laid an idea on me to go and learn hand-to-hand combat. What this translated to was going to sit with the kids on a one-on-one. As He does, God had already made arrangements for it to be possible. I was still on the stress leave from work. The stipulation of course was that I go for counseling, and God had me covered there too—the fellow I met with was a born-again Christian, so we did a lot of praying, which helped more than any "talk session" would have.

So armed with my new idea from God, equipped with the time off work, I went to the avenue where all the kids hung out. Now, how to get them to come and talk with me? I did all that I could think of. I bought a couple packs of smokes and put them on the table beside me and my coffee, knowing these kids were broke and would come ask for one. Put your religious judgment aside. Kids were going to hell, and I used what I could think of to get them to come to hear about Jesus. I was more concerned about kids going to hell than about whether or not smoking was acceptable.

One by one, they would come. "Can I bum a smoke?"

"Sure," I'd say. And I'd offer to buy them coffee if they would sit and chat with me. It didn't take long before they would automatically come, and I would talk to them about Jesus and where their lives were heading without Him, and how happy and loved they would be with Him.

My dad started coming, and took it a step further—he would buy them a complete lunch if they would sit with him and talk. He even had some kids coming that were older, one in particular raised in a Christian home who had deep questions for my dad. My dad never failed to give answers that satisfied this would-be scholar, and would point to Jesus again.

After a while, all the kids knew I was Nadine's mom, and that Henry was Nadine's grandpa. I'm not sure this helped Nadine's stories of why she'd run away, or how "bad" it was at home, but my mission was simple—to hurt and destroy the dark side, and steal out of their demonic clutches as many kids as possible. Whether or not this would bring Nadine back I didn't know, but I was bent on war.

I found out there was a group of kids involved in their own form of Satanism. I learned that there was an older fellow named George leading this ragtag band. These kids were scared of him, and yet marveled at his supposed power. This angered me beyond belief. Having been on both sides of the fence, I could appreciate what they saw as power, yet I knew Jesus crushed it and was in fact the power source. How was I to get this across to the kids?

George was in the coffee place a few tables away; he had his band of ragtags, and I had the few at my table listening to me talk about God. Suddenly I had an idea (okay, the Holy Spirit *gave* me an idea). I always carried oil in little vials with me to anoint things, so I said to the kids, "This is oil that I've prayed over and asked God to be present in—watch the power of God."

I put just a drop or two on my fingers and walked past George's table on the pretext of going to the bathroom. I took the finger that I had placed the oil on and touched his shoulder, saying "Hi."

On my way back from the washroom, I watched as he squirmed and tugged at his coat where I had placed the anointed oil. This wasn't lost on the kids at my table; they couldn't believe it! I reiterated that the power of the living God was nothing to be trifled with, and that whatever power George had was no match. By now, over the weeks I'd been there I'd also given the kids a crash course on the demonic and how it operated to steal and destroy their lives. They were watching firsthand.

The demons in and around George were well aware of what was going on, and he was becoming more agitated. I went over to his table to talk to him. He was putting on the demonic "I'm so strong" show that they use to try to scare or impress humans, but God pushed me on. I started praying against him and his power, and I told him his demonic jewelry was offensive and had to go. I took oil and placed it on his chains; he couldn't rip them off himself fast enough! He threw them at the table and glared at me. We had an audience of kids watching this, and—truth be told—I was scared, but I kept praying in my mind, "God, show yourself to these kids, remove him from his pedestal, and show them that *You* are all powerful."

George and I began an angry conversation—him declaring he had the power, me declaring God had the power. Out of my mouth flew these words: "I challenge you to a fight to the death! You can try to put a death curse on me, but the blood of Jesus will cause it to bounce back to you, and you will die. If you really believe you're stronger, prove it!"

Now, in hindsight, I don't know if it was my own headstrong anger or God having had enough, but thankfully God is not only full of grace but truly full of power, and He used those words. The kids were taken aback, George was speech-less, and I, though trembling on the inside, kept a brave face. God would either save me, or I would die; it was up to God and God alone.

George didn't place any curse (that I'm aware of), but he did leave in a hurry. Before he managed to leave the place, I also warned him that my daughter had better not be part of his group or I'd be praying even more trouble on him. I'd love to report that the kids—after witnessing the absolute power of the living and loving God I was telling them about—all re-pented and came to Jesus. No, this did not happen, but I know that God doesn't waste anything, and this day and its events will forever be with them, so perhaps one day they will come to a living relationship with Jesus.

In time, Nadine did come home. She of course brought her many demons with her, but my baby was home, and I was praising God that she was alive. She still hung out with her troubled friends and wasn't attending school, but she was home.

Interestingly, her friends (troubled themselves) would call me to tell me how "scary'" Nadine was, and how they couldn't quite explain the feeling that sometimes came over them when she was around. Again, I used this opportunity to tell them about the reality of demons and the ultimate power and love of Jesus.

Nadine had been dating a fellow named James. While Na-dine was out with her friends one night, I went to the coffee shop yet again. I ran into James, who had a rather beaten-up face; when I asked him what had happened, he explained that his dad had beaten him up. I was beside myself! How could a parent do this kind of damage to their own child?

"You're coming to live with us!" I announced, without having given it any thought or prayer. Edward tried to warn me it was a bad idea, but stubborn as I was, I wouldn't listen.

Against Edward's wishes and much better judgment, James moved in with us. I put him in a room in the basement, while Nadine and the rest of us lived upstairs. This went on for a couple of months. Nadine and James were both looking for work or discussing the possibility of going to school—in other words, they did nothing, but had a comfortable place to live and food to eat. I had gone back to work by now, so they were on their own during the day...

Yeah, you guessed it. Truly, what did I expect to happen? Sometimes, we can have the right intentions yet make things worse by lending a helping hand. Ask the guys who tried to do the right thing by grabbing the Ark of God so it wouldn't fall—they ended up dead (see 2 Samuel 6).

Chapter Twenty-Two

Another event happened during this time: we heard about a fellow by the name of Bernie doing deliverance in Calgary, just a few short hours away. Nadine was manifesting her demons so often that even James would sometimes be a little concerned about her. My folks bought Nadine and me a plane ticket to Calgary; I was taking her for deliverance whether she wanted it or not! I'd had enough of the nonsense. Once and for all, this was going to get dealt with. My only hope was that she would accept Christ rather than end up seven times worse.

Getting to the plane and on it was an event in itself. Nadine dressed in her darkest of dark clothes, her face a permanent evil scowl and extremely vile. When we landed in Calgary, her demons tried a different spin—Nadine was nice and mellow, asking to go shopping and just spend time together talking (spending time with her when she actually wanted to be with me was something I always cherished), but this time I was on a mission and wouldn't be dissuaded.

When we arrived at Bernie's office, Nadine was radiating hate and evil again. I sat with them for a bit, and I noticed Nadine squeezing a glass bottle in her hands. *I bet she would like to smash it on his head*, I thought, so of course I prayed against it. After a time, I left them alone to continue the deliverance.

This wasn't a showy, loud, yelling kind; it was quieter and laid-back, but the results were the same.

When they walked out of Bernie's office, I saw something I hadn't seen in years—my daughter. Her eyes were bright, she had a smile on her face, and she was actually laughing. The transformation was amazing!

Bernie did warn her: "Get plugged into a church, get with God, stay away from your old ways, because those demons will be wanting to come back, and they are not happy with you."

This is the one key part of deliverance—the name of Jesus holds all power; no demon on Earth can stand against Jesus. That's absolute power, but if the delivered person walks away from this then it's full-blown "hell to pay." Sort of like a kid on the playground getting his stronger big brother to push away the other little kids harassing him; if he leaves the protection of the big brother, the little kids come back, even angrier, to get revenge.

Nadine did promise to heed the warning. She was different. I hadn't seen her actually happy, fun, and full of joy in so long that I felt like she was almost a stranger. She very badly wanted to go shopping to ditch the horrible, dark, evil clothes she was wearing and replace them with something nice. Yes, this I could get behind. We had such a happy afternoon talking, laughing, shopping, and discussing a future that for her was now bright; for once she had hopes and dreams. I also asked her about why, when she was in with Bernie, she had been squeezing the glass bottle so hard.

She replied, "I wanted to break it and smash it on his head. I don't know what stopped me."

I knew—God had shown me, and I had prayed.

The plane ride back was amazingly different! She was laughing and joking all the way back, and I was in heaven! When we got home, Edward immediately noticed a difference, but more interestingly, it was James who noticed the most. After spending a day with Nadine, and after she'd gone to bed, James came up to talk. He was visibly shaken up and really dumbfounded. I asked him what was wrong, and what I heard made my heart jump for joy!

His words: "I don't know what to say; Nadine is so different! I can't explain it. She's just different! I don't understand what happened; there's something different about her. You can even see it in her eyes."

I was so excited I wanted to scream, but instead I went on to once again explain salvation, Jesus and His love, the demonic and how real it was, and yet how powerful Jesus was, and that simply put, Nadine had had deliverance and was a new creation.

He was still in shock and said, "Your God can do this? Your God can really do this?" He said he needed some time to mull this all over, and went back to his room.

Of course, I thought he'd immediately become a Christian because—by his own words—he'd never seen such a thing and had acknowledged God's power. Of *course* he would accept Christ that night. Right?

Wrong! Instead, what happened is something common not only in the Bible but in today's world. James had witnessed the power of the living God, Nadine had been set free and was truly happy, and rather than embrace God and come into a whole new life they dismissed, excused away, and took for granted what had happened, and slowly and gradually returned to the pig slop. *"Of them the proverbs are true: 'A dog returns to its vomit,' and, 'A sow that is washed returns to her wallowing in the mud'"* (2 Peter 2:22).

Sadly, while Nadine was enjoying her newfound freedom, she took no steps closer to Christ, so rather than experience a continuation of freedom, happiness, and love, she took the well-traveled path back to her folly. A short time after the Calgary encounter, I found out the kids had been having sex in my house! With this shocking revelation—yes, my head was so far in the sand I could see China!—I decided to tell James he had to leave. I told him I'd pay for a hotel for a couple nights, but after that he'd have to deal with where to live on his own.

His reaction was unexpected. He swore at me, called me names and gave me the finger while his parents picked him up. His parents? I let him stay with us so he could avoid his home situation, and yet here they were picking him up, and I was the bad guy. Nadine wasn't sad to see him go; she was actually a little relieved. Having a boyfriend was one thing; having him around 24-7 wasn't as enjoyable as she'd thought.

A week or so later, we were having a chilled-back family night. We went to grab pizza for all of us, and Nadine ran into the drugstore. We went home armed with pizza, and picked the movies we were going to watch. While we were getting things ready, Nadine was doing her own thing in the bathroom. A few minutes later she came out with the announcement, "I'm pregnant!"

No wonder she'd stopped at the drugstore. This wasn't something she'd planned for, nor was it something I'd expected. Yes, even though I'd allowed the opportunity for this to happen, it still took me by surprise. My husband, on the other hand, was in more of an angry "I told you so" mode.

Nadine's pregnancy took a toll on an already strained marriage. We had already mentally gone different ways; we had separated previously a couple times, and spiritually we were perhaps on the same page but of a different book. Edward's plan was that Nadine would give the baby up for adoption; after all, she was too screwed up to raise a child. Okay, no argument there. But having been pregnant at an early age myself, I knew she would have to make the decision herself, or she would forever blame us for what may come.

Near the end of her pregnancy, she decided she would in fact be keeping the baby. I was both thrilled and scared. Edward and I once again separated, this time for good—not entirely due to Nadine's pregnancy; it was just the catalyst for the inevitable.

Nadine had her baby, an adorable little boy. We had already furnished a room for him (with the help of my parents), and life was continuing on. Nadine worked at whatever jobs were handy at the time: gas station, retail, before landing a permanent job at a bagel shop. It was convenient; her shop was close to where I worked, so we would meet for lunch and sometimes go home together. Parker, her son, was in daycare. From a worldly stance, it looked like things were beginning to stabilize. Nadine was steady enough in her job that she moved to the basement suite. By now, my grandfather had passed away, and Nadine and I had been living in the upstairs of the house (where he had lived) while my folks were renting out the basement suite. The fellow below moved out, so Nadine moved in. Seemed perfect—we lived together, yet had our own places.

However, the pull of her old lifestyle started becoming more and more evident; after having had deliverance once and then returning to her old lifestyle, she now had even more demons actively playing with her mind. This time they weren't as obvious; they had learned to be a little less blatant and belligerent. Nadine would go out late at night and of course I would babysit; I wasn't going to have her dragging my beautiful grandson out. He was too special. Out she would go and sometimes she'd return in the late hours—other times, not till the next day. Through this, though, she maintained a job and at least the appearance of normality. Because things looked normal on the outside, it was easier for me to sit back. Although I knew deep down things were a total spiritual mess, if I focused on only the outward appearance, I could lull myself into believing everything would be alright.

As Christians, we do too much of this, the focusing on the outward; we judge people as "sinners" based on their outward appearance, and every bit as stupidly and wrongly, we also assume all is well and folks are "good Christians" if they appear that way. Thankfully, God judges by what is not seen—the state of our hearts.

One morning while I had Parker upstairs (because Nadine had been out the night before), I had a sick feeling that I couldn't shake—something wasn't right. I prayed, but it wouldn't go away. I finally ventured downstairs, where I knocked on and opened the door. From the door there was a clear view into the living room; all I saw was a man's head pop up and look somewhat embarrassed.

I turned to go back upstairs, knowing full well what had been going on. Nadine came up shortly, angry that I had walked in on her and caused her friend to leave so abruptly. Before she came up, I had been chatting with a friend about all this. My friend was a Christian and she said to "tell Nadine it's going to be a girl."

After Nadine's rant about my interruption I told her, "By the way, you're pregnant now and going to have a girl."

She laughed, but I knew my friend's words were prophetic.

Sure enough, by the time Parker was a little over a year old, Nadine had another baby, a girl, exactly as God had said. Her name was Gabriella.

Once again, a demon lord approached the throne of God and bowed (as every knee must bow in His presence).

"They are born. We have rights to them, and this time we will have them," snarled the hideous creature.

"No, they belong to me," declared the Lord of Hosts.

"We will unleash all of hell's fury. This time, they will not escape our storm." The demon, in his satanic pride, truly believed this time he would accomplish the mission.

Jesus laughed. He, the Holy Spirit, and God the Father, all in one, knew full well the outcome. Because of the cross and its victory—through my new freedom, knowledge of all Truth, and living relationship with Jesus—*I* would be the next, far more powerful, storm the demons would deal with. There would be battles to be fought, but the victory was assured.

Final Words

A child walked along a beach that was covered in stranded starfish. She scooped up as many as she could fit in her hands and ran to the ocean to put them back in and save them. A by-stander yelled, "Don't bother! There are too many. You can't save them all; it doesn't matter!"

The child, placing another into the ocean, replied, "But it does matter to this one," and she continued on.

If this book has made a difference to you, and you are one of those starfish, I would love to know. If you have questions or comments, I would love to chat.

Email me at kimmieishappy@live.com.

www.demonicstorm.com

About the Author

Kimmie lives with her daughter, granddaughter, and extended family (two dogs and two cats) in Alberta, Canada. She enjoys gardening and being politically incorrect in wishing everyone Merry Christmas, which she starts to do in late summer.

Those who know her enjoy her humor and light approach to life, as well as her ever-present sarcasm. She loves to play the role of the jester, as laughter is key to who she is. Her other side is a fierce and tenacious prayer warrior determined to tear down strongholds and see captives set free—to expose and destroy demonic trappings and see Jesus' truth bring freedom. Her motto, encompassing both sides of her personality, is "Live your life in such a way that when your feet hit the floor, Satan shudders and says "[Oh crap!] She's awake.""[2]

---

2 Kristina Smith, *Thoughts from God's Favorite Child* (Bloomington, IN: AuthorHouse, 2012), p. 11.

www.ingramcontent.com/pod-product-compliance
Lightning Source LLC
Chambersburg PA
CBHW062113080426
42734CB00012B/2849